PHILPO

LHP

Dan River Basin Association

DRBA Headquarters
413 Church Street
Suite 401
Eden, NC 27288
Phone: 336.627.6270

DRBA Martinsville & Henry County
3300 Kings Mountain Rd
PO Box 7
Collinsville, VA 24078
Phone: 276.634.2545

Nancy Bell
PO Box 942
Rocky Mount, VA 24151

Published by Tom Perry's Laurel Hill Publishing LLC
P. O. Box 11
4443 Ararat Highway
Ararat, VA 24053
276.692.5300
freestateofpatrick@yahoo.com
www.freestateofpatrick.com

Philpott Stories

By Nancy Bell

**For The
Dan River Basin Association**

Cover photo by Linda Drage.
Title page photo courtesy of the *James Ramsey Collection.*

ISBN-13: 978-1507781531

ISBN-10: 1507781539

Dedication

This book is dedicated to the US Army Corps of Engineers at Philpott Lake, keepers of the pristine natural beauty of the area and the safety of the dam, ramps and trails that make recreational activities safe.

One hundred percent of the proceeds of this book support the stewardship fund at the Dan River Basin Association, a regional nonprofit that preserves and promotes the recreational and cultural assets of the Dan River Basin. www.drba.org

Dan River Basin Association

Mission

The Dan River Basin Association preserves and promotes the natural and cultural resources of the <u>Dan River Basin</u> through stewardship, recreation and education.

Vision

The Dan River Basin Association envisions an economically vibrant bi-state community with a regional identity, where people enjoy easy access to healthy rivers, parks, trails and heritage attractions.

Goals

The Dan River Basin Association works to: preserve the river corridor with a series of municipal, county, and state parks and trails; increase public access to rivers; build constituency for the rivers and outdoor recreation through monthly outings; protect water quality by instituting stream monitoring across the Basin; promote regional nature and heritage tourism; and bridge boundaries to create a bi-state borderland community.

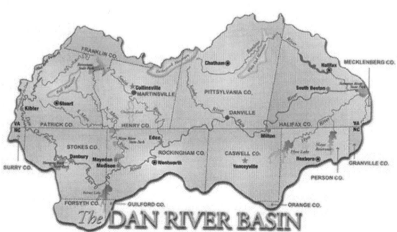

The Dan River Basin Association has four key program areas:

- **Stewardship**
Promote stewardship by encouraging policies and practices that support healthy water and clean air throughout the Dan River Basin.
- **Recreation**
Improve opportunities for river- and trail-based recreation throughout the Dan River Basin.
- **Education**
Provide education and outreach regarding the history and significance of the natural and cultural treasures of the Dan River Basin and the importance of restoring and preserving these resources.
- **Regional Identity**
Promote a regional identity and support regional tourism based on the shared river heritage of communities throughout the Dan River Basin.

The Dan River crosses the North Carolina-Virginia state line eight times on its way from the Blue Ridge Mountains to John H. Kerr Reservoir. The 3300-square-mile Dan River Basin comprises approximately one-third of the Roanoke River Basin. Major tributaries of the Dan River are the Mayo, Smith, Sandy, Banister, and Hyco Rivers.

The Dan River Basin includes all or most of eight counties: Patrick, Henry, Pittsylvania, and Halifax in Virginia, and Stokes, Rockingham, Caswell and Person in North Carolina. Smaller portions of eight more counties lie in the Dan River Basin: Floyd, Franklin, and Mecklenburg in Virginia, and Surry, Forsyth, Guilford, Orange, and Granville in North Carolina.

Outdoor enthusiasts and concerned citizens organized the Dan River Basin Association in 2002 to preserve and promote the wilderness-like rivers of this border region of Piedmont North Carolina and Virginia. Faced with the decline of tobacco and textiles, our traditional economic bases, leaders in the Basin's counties recognize the increasing importance of the abundant high-quality water in this 3300-square-mile region. In addition to its economic value as a water source and its historical significance as a means of transportation, this river system ca provide excellent recreational opportunities to the 1.5 million citizens who live within an hour's drive.

The Association's founders are promoting the rivers for multipl uses, including recreation and commercial and municipal growth. We believe that, with careful planning, natural and cultural preservation and economic development can occur hand-in-hand. The unspoiled rivers, the region's unique and greatest resource, will be at the center a the sixteen counties of the Basin build a diverse economy, which must be based in part on new ideas. The Dan River Basin Association believe that providing outdoor recreation is essential to the region's quality of life and its ability to draw new investment.

The Dan River Basin Association is a 501(c) (3) nonprofit organization incorporated in North Carolina and Virginia, with basin-wide membership and directors representing both states, and offices and professional staff in Collinsville, Virginia and Eden, North Carolina.

Contents

Author's Note

13

Introduction

15

PART ONE

Native American are First Residents of Philpott Area

21

Belcher Keeps History of Native American Forebearers Alive

23

Native American Descendant's Family Lived in Land under Philpott

29

Gravely Excavations Reveal Ancient Indian Life at Philpott

33

PART TWO

The History Keepers Recall Tales of Land under Philpott
and Fairy Stone Lakes

37

Once Bustling Town Thrived Under Fairy Stone and Philpott Lakes

39

Miller's Granddaughter Is Keeper of Lake History

53

Flood Catches Local Woman's Father, Others

59

Surveyor Recalls Wildness of the Area before Construction, Interacting
with the People

65

The Miller and His Family Live Through the Great Depression

69

Growing Up In a School House: Carter Descendants Recall a Tough but Happy Life
73

Historians and Residents Gather in 2013 to Remember Life before Philpott and Fairy Stone Lakes
75

Philpott Lake: What Is In a Name?
79

Descendants of Albert Buchanan Philpott and Mary Elizabeth Helms Philpott Recall Rich Family History
81

Philpott Project: Timeline at a Glance
89

CCC Makes Reservoir Building Possible at Nearby Fairy Stone Lake
111

PART THREE
The Moonshine Economy
113

Newsman Documents Decades of Illegal Liquor Making
115

DeHart Family Well Known For Distilling Spirits
119

Flatfooting and Moonshining Way of Life for Hodges
125

PART FOUR
Keepers of the Lake: U. S. Army Corps of Engineers Maintains the Dam Ensures Safety
127

Rockwell Says Philpott about Natural Beauty and Economic Development
129

Park Ranger Shares the Philpott Story
133
Yesterday's Features, Today
137
Ten Fast Facts about Philpott Dam
141

Sources
143

Index
147

Before there was a lake, there was a town named Philpott.
(Charles and Jo Anne Philpott)

Author's Note

At the request of the Dan River Basin Association, I began this book as a history of the area around – and under, Philpott Lake. I dragged out maps, poked around online, and interviewed those whose names kept popping up. I sorted through dusty archives and spent many wonderful hours combing the areas around the lake, finding beauty around every bend, and kayaking its nooks and crannies. I met some interesting people and made some new friends. In the process, the story became less about history and more about the people, alive now, whose memories tell the story of what life was like before reservoir building flooded the area creating the beautiful mountain lake that exists today. You will read about a surveyor, a miller's daughter, a moonshiner, and several who lost family members to floods along the Smith River before Philpott Dam was built. You will meet a Native American descendant of the area and an historian. You will hear from the US Army Corps of Engineers who manage the dam. You will hear about their stories, but many others remain to be told. So we pose this challenge: to make this a living, breathing project onto which others can add their recollections, share their photographs and keep the story alive. DRBA has created a link on www.danriver.org where you can add your knowledge and memories of Philpott now and then. Please use it to help tell the Philpott Lake story and visit often to see what has been added.

To those who have let me into their homes, allowed me to pilfer their precious photos, taken me on fieldtrips, corrected my assumptions, rendezvoused for coffee, and met me at the end of dirt roads to exchange photos, maps and memories – thank you. I have enjoyed getting to know each of you and hope our paths cross many more times around the beautiful Philpott Lake. --Nancy Bell

Before there was a lake, there were people, who left their mark.
(Charles and Jo Anne Philpott)

Rosa Barnes, Philpott, Virginia, Post Mistress (Martinsville Bulletin)

Introduction

For those who lived along the Smith River in the Piedmont of Virginia before 1950, floods were an accepted fact of life – the price paid for living and farming in the beautiful Blue Ridge Mountains. Once crisscrossed with Native American paths, villages, and hunting grounds, the region evolved into thriving logging, mining and mill towns -- followed by one of the most prosperous moonshine trades in the United States before and during the time of Prohibition.

The people who called the rugged land of tall mountains and deep hollows around Franklin, Henry, and Patrick counties home during the Great Depression both relied upon and feared the mighty Smith River. A downpour could cause a flash flood and roaring river water upstream often meant serious flooding in the rich lowlands along the Smith. It was not until the Great Flood of 1937 – a devastating act of nature during which lives and property were lost (and the nearby towns of Bassett and Philpott were swallowed up in brown, debris-laden river water), that the idea of taming the Smith River was seriously considered.

Based on a Federal Power Commission study, it was recommended in 1946 that a concrete dam with a powerhouse be constructed on the Smith River. It was a logical place because of the mountainous terrain and deep hollows. While this would mean flooding an area inhabited by generations of families, the dam would serve several important functions. In addition to flood control, it would generate electric power and put local men to work in good paying construction jobs. For the families living there, it also meant leaving their ancestral farms and businesses for higher ground.

The Smith River and the many creeks that feed into it, routinely caused loss of life and property by flooding during sustained rains or snowmelt. Historic photos show the town of Bassett (VA) awash in floodwaters from the untamed Smith River, and unconfirmed family stories tell of youngsters and livestock swallowed by sudden rushing

The town of Bassett was often flooded before Philpott Dam was constructed. *(US Army Corps of Engineers)*

water, which could briefly be heard in the distance before roaring through the low lands, and snatching everything it reached in its wake.

In 1948, the banks of the Smith River near the construction site were cleared and an access road from State Route 57 to the Henry County side of the river was completed. Included was an overlook, which provided a bird's eye view of construction and later a spectacular view of the new reservoir below. An engineer's office followed the next year along with an additional access road. By March of 1950, workers were on the job, and the first of many loads of concrete was poured.

The project proceeded mostly on time, but not without incident. Several weeks after concrete work was started, the Smith River broke through the cofferdam and inundated the excavated area around the dam. A contractor's crane and several pumps were lost to the rushing water, and the cofferdam area had to be reconstructed. Another flash flood, four months later, did less damage but secured the notion that the dam was critically needed.

This popular foot bridge connected Bassett Furniture Company to workers who lived on the other side of the Smith River and was a popular route to and from work at the plant. It, too, eventually fell to flooding. *(US Army Corps of Engineers)*

With construction of the Philpott Dam in the late 1940s early 1950s, low lying areas were no longer at risk of flash flooding. A new kind of flood came – one that required the people who lived there to abandon their homes, crops and businesses, and head to higher ground. This flood was deliberate and now covers 3,000 acres of mountain valleys. The approximately 52-billion-gallon lake is surrounded by 7,000 acres of forested land that is managed by the U.S. Army Corps of Engineers.

Small parks and campgrounds dot the perimeter. The area is a popular destination for fishing, hiking, boating, camping, photography, the study of natural history, and exploring. The US Army Corps of Engineers (Wilmington District) maintains a visitor center there, and nearby Fairy Stone State Park is but one of its "destination connections" in the Philpott Lake area that contribute to its rich history. Adjoining Philpott Lake is Fairy Stone State Park with nearly 5,000 acres of predominately forested land, another 5,500 acres of Virginia Department of Game and Inland Fisheries forest, and its own small lake with a beach and cabins.

What lies beneath the waters of Philpott and Fairy Stone lakes a fascinating history of homes razed, people (some reluctantly) relocated, graves moved, and drowned railroad tracks. This is an attempt to describe the history of the area through the accounts of families who lived there while also describing how Philpott Dam changed the landscape forever. What follows are a few of the stories of people who lived in the area (or whose family members did) before the reservoir was created, of those who worked on the project or of those who lost land, or loved ones, or who are simply fascinated with the area and how drastically the landscape changed forever.

Before the lake, the Smith River unleashed its power downstream.

The Bridge at Fieldale, Virginia, under flood.
(US Army Corps of Engineers)

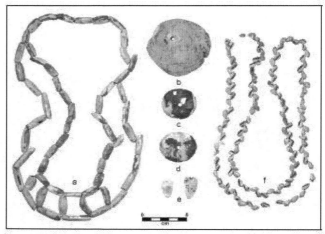

Figure 28. Shell artifacts from the Philpott site: necklace made of columella and whelk-shoulder beads from Burial 3 (the configuration of the beads on strand is conjecture) (a); gorget (b), oval disks (c), and drilled shell triangles (d) from Burial 5; and marginella beads from Burial 3 (f).

(Courtesy of the Archaeology Lab, University of North Carolina)

Fairy Stones dot the area around Philpott and Fairy Stone Lakes.

PART ONE
Native Americans are First Residents of Philpott Area

Douglas Belcher holds one of the beautiful hand crafted baskets from his collection. *(Nancy Bell)*

Belcher Keeps History of Native American Forbearers Alive
Cherokee Blessing

May the warm winds of Heaven blow softly on your home,
And the Great Spirit bless all who enter there.
May your moccasins make happy tracks in many snows,
And may the rainbow always touch your shoulder.

Douglas Belcher spreads out his collection of baskets, pottery, and other Native American artifacts on two long tables at the Virginia Museum of Natural History. Each piece has a story to tell, and as he unwraps the precious objects, he talks with a great deal of respect about the people who made them. He can describe how the baskets were made, of what materials, from which period of history they derive, and the techniques for creating some of the strongest and most beautiful items. Included in the collection are photographs of present day Native Americans and their descendants, still working the crafts of their ancestors in the traditional manner.

Belcher, retired from a textile company, former history teacher, and amateur archeologist from Martinsville, is the keeper of Native American history in the area and a descendant of native people, as well. Regarded locally as an expert on Native American baskets and pottery, he has acquired a large collection, with some pieces on display at the Bassett Historical Center and others having been displayed at the Virginia Museum of Natural History.

Belcher uses the artifacts to tell the captivating story of the native peoples who once inhabited the area around Philpott, now under water.

Philpott Area Indian History, as told by Douglas Belcher:

While it remains unclear the exact names of the tribes who inhabited the rich riverside areas of the Smith River, they most likely were of Saura, a.k.a. Saraw, a.k.a. Cheraw, a.k.a SE-RA-TEE / Catawba Indian origin. Sa-rak means tall grass or river cane. This group of Indians are referred to as "people of the tall grass," according to Frank G. Speck

23

of the University of Pennsylvania. The Dan River was called the Saura River as early as 1673.

Native Americans Traveled Trail Bisecting Town of Philpott

The Tutelo-Saura Path once ran from modern Pennsylvania to Georgia. Coming from the Tutelo town in the Roanoke Valley, it passed through the Saura town at Philpott, crossed the Smith River at the Great Indian Fields, passed through a Saura town on the Mayo River, entered North Carolina, and led to the large Upper Sauratown village and crossed the Dan River.

The trail has been referred to by many names -- Warrior's Path, Iroquois War Trail, and the Carolina Road, for example. It was considered a vital artery for trading and was used by the aggressive Iroquois to ambush Virginia Indians during the 1670s. Settlers also used the trail during the 1700s as they began to traverse and move into the area.

Indian Towns Dotted the Smith River

Goblintown was a village which is now under the waters of Philpott Lake, and it was also referred to as Peach Tree Bottom. A 1774 land survey noted that the native people had planted and maintained peach groves in the area. Goblintown Creek flows in the north of Patrick County. Across the Smith River, Bone Bottom was a larger Indian settlement so named by the Europeans because of the number and variety of animal bones and fresh water shells found there. Additionally English traders from the James River settlements traded objects of European origin -- glass beads, nails, gun flints, etc. These villages are in addition to the Town Creek (Buttram-Town Creek) settlement, a.k.a. the Philpott Archaeological Site where glass, copper and brass objects were found in abundance. Cherokee Indians claimed most of the land in southwest Virginia in the 1700s. Additionally, the Smith River National Register of Historic Places Rockshelter District contains 15 rock shelters in the upper Smith River Valley. Six of these are situated at the Philpott Reservoir -- all containing cultural remains.

First Europeans Enter the Area

The area now covered by Fairy Stone and Philpott Lakes once was part of Lunenburg and Halifax Counties. During the French & Indian War (1756-1763), the area was raided by Indian tribes from the Ohio Valley. In 1758, war parties of Shawnee, Delaware, Wyandotte, and Mingo Indians formed three groups to attack settlers. One of the attacks, at the head of Goblintown Creek, resulted in the kidnapping of settlers Isham Bernat (Barnett) and Robert Pusey, who lived near Otter Creek on the Smith River. The prisoners were taken on the long journey to Fort Detroit, where they were delivered to the French. Some would later return home. Five years later, the Workman family farm at Goblintown Creek was burned by Indian invaders, and many horses were captured.

By 1768, much of the land east of the New River in southwest Virginia was sold by the Cherokee to the British government. Western Patrick County and parts of Carroll and Floyd Counties were included in the transaction.

.

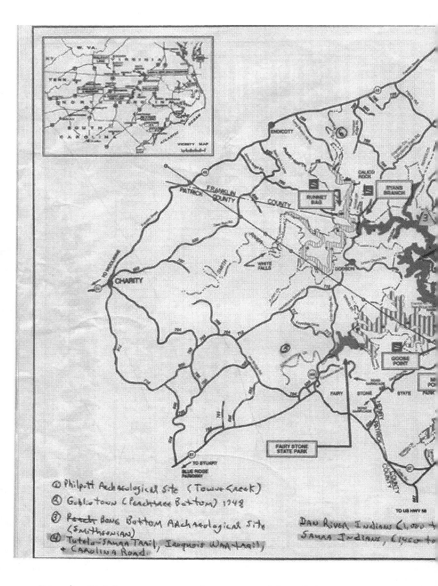

Douglas Belcher uses a modern map of the Philpott Lake area to illustrate important Native American landmarks of the past.

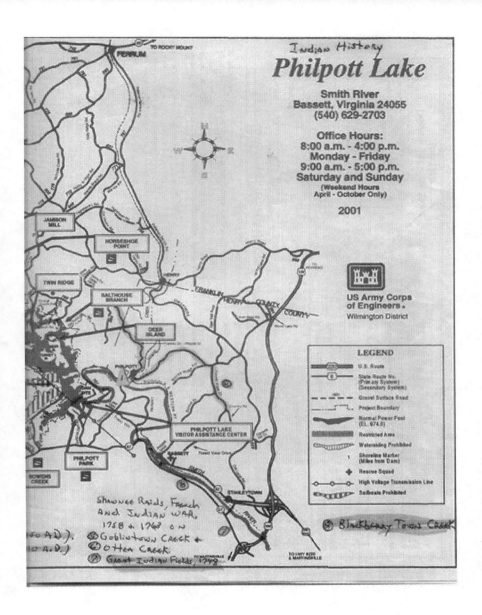

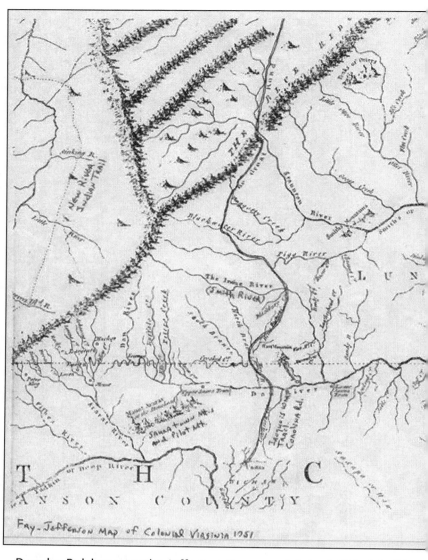

Douglas Belcher uses the Jefferson-Fry map of Colonial Virginia from 1751 to illustrate the movements of Indians. *(Douglas Belcher)*

Native American Descendant's Family Lived in Land under Philpott

At nearly 90 years of age, Eunice Kirkman's hair is striped with gray but mostly still the dark strands of her Native American ancestry. Kirkman is a descendant of Cheraw and Cherokee tribes in and around Patrick County and very determined that the history of the native people be preserved and shared.

From her desk at the Patrick County Historical Society, where she continues to work several days per week, she answers all kinds of questions about the history of the rugged mountain land known as Patrick County. But her favorite questions are those about the Native Americans who once lived in the area. She has been researching the Indian genealogy of the area for many years. It is sketchy, she says, because of the stigma once attached to being an Indian. Many native people moved away or hid their heritage for their own safety, she said.

Kirkman's grandmother lived at Bowen's Creek before the area was flooded, and Kirkman's mother, Louanna Baliles Robertson "mourned the loss of the family home until the day she died," Kirkman said. It was Louanna who ordered the family graves moved to higher ground when the area was lost to what is now Philpott Lake. Sharing one's Indian heritage was not always the smart thing to do, she said.

"A Dr. Plecker was in charge of vital statistics, and he claimed that all Indians in Virginia were either white or black," she said. Walter Ashby Plecker was a physician and public health advocate who was the first registrar of Virginia's Bureau of Vital Statistics, serving from 1912-1946. He drafted and lobbied for the passage of the Racial Integrity Act of 1924 by the Virginia legislature. He believed that no Indians existed in Virginia. He did not allow the census to show Indians as a race. Natives went into hiding after that, said Kirkman, describing a time when to be found out was dangerous. Any dark-skinned people were said to be African American in descent and treated accordingly, she remembered. It was better to be listed as white.

Mary Jane Hagood, Native-American descendant.
(Patrick County Historical Society)

Louanna Baliles Robertson was Eunice Kirkman's grandmother. She saw
that ancestral graves were moved to higher ground before the water
rose. *(Patrick County Historical Society)*

"We lost our history. You didn't dare tell anyone you were Indian," shared Kirkman. " Some of her family and tribe members stayed hidden. Others joined the Monacan tribe near Lynchburg, who welcomed them from the oppressive Plecker, Kirkman said.

Earlier, in 1938, as part of Plecker's reign, Indians in the area were rounded up and sent to Oklahoma carrying only the clothes on their backs. "Patrick County's white people protected as many as they could," Kirkman said, estimating that about 1,200 escaped relocation leaving on their own or by staying in hiding in the county's remote mountainous areas. In some cases, white neighbors claimed them as family members, she said.

Kirkman was one of the first Native Americans in the area to claim her ancestry on both sides of her family through DNA testing. On her mother's Cheraw side, Kirkman's family can be traced back to the settlement at Philpott on the grounds of Bassett Mirror Company that was excavated by Richard Gravely in the 1980s. The excavation produced pottery, weapons and other artifacts as well as Spanish trading beads. More information about this follows.

Eunice Kirkman poses beside the ceremonial dress she wore in numerous local Pow Wow celebrations. *(Nancy Bell)*

The late Richard P. Gravely, Jr. of Martinsville is shown visiting with Catawba Indian pottery maker, Doris Blue, and her family in 1983. Gravely discovered the Philpott Archaeological site on the Smith River in the 1960s. *(Courtesy of the Archaeology Lab, University of North Carolina, Chapel Hill)*

Gravely Excavations Reveal Ancient Indian Life at Philpott, Evidence of Early Trade with Europeans

Richard P. Gravely, Jr., of Martinsville, was an industrialist, a civic leader, a historian and an archeologist who studied Indian villages along the Smith and Mayo Rivers from the 1960s – 1980s. He was honored with the title of Virginia Archeologist of the Year in 1984, based largely on his work at Philpott that produced 90,000 artifacts. Today, the Richard P. Gravely, Jr. Nature Preserve features more than 500 acres of riverside walking trails and much of the flora and fauna Gravely loved. Gravely purchased the land, a former plantation and tobacco farm, and donated it for the purpose of preserving it when he died in 1988. He also left Research Laboratories of Archaeology at the University of North Carolina, Chapel Hill, funds to support further archeological investigations.

Richard Gravely, Jr. and members of the Patrick Henry Chapter of the Archeology Society of Virginia first recorded the area where Bassett Mirror now stands in Philpott (VA) as a Native American archaeological site in 1965. The rich soil parallel to the Smith River proved rich in artifacts as well, and it was excavated again in 1972, from 1974-76, and again in 1985 producing over 90,000 artifacts. The excavations, heaviest from 1974-76 when Bassett Mirror was being built, revealed at least 25 archeological features: 22 burials, two palisade ditches – evidence of a substantial late prehistoric village of the Dan River phase.

In 1985, several features were discovered adjacent to the earlier excavation area. Four of these – two pits and two burial sites containing European trade beads, were salvaged by Gravely. Collectively, the archaeological data from the Philpott site indicate that it was occupied sporadically until the Dan River phase, when a large, palisaded village was established. Large quantities of artifacts at the site indicate that this village stood for a relatively long period of time.

The Philpott site is significant because it represents one of the primary Dan River phase settlements in the upper Smith River valley and is one of only a few sites in the region that has produced evidence of Indian-European contact.

Catawba Indian pottery maker Sarah Harris is shown with her grandchildren at her home on the Catawba Indian Reservation. The Harris family descend from the Saura (Cheraw) Indians who inhabited the area around Philpott Lake.
(Courtesy of the Library of Congress)

Figure 4. View of the 1974–1976 excavation area showing partially backfilled squares.

(Courtesy of the Archaeology Lab, University of North Carolina)

The Turner Family of Patrick County during a corn shucking around Philpott Lake. *(Patrick County Historical Society)*

PART TWO

The History Keepers Recall Tales of Land Under Philpott and Fairy Stone Lakes

Above, the beach at Fairy Stone Park, which covers the town of Fayerdale. Below, Goblintown Creek, which feeds Fairy Stone Lake is near an opening to Fayerdale's iron ore mines. *(Nancy Bell)*

Once Bustling Town Thrived Under Fairy Stone, Philpott Lakes

Adjacent to Philpott Lake is Fairy Stone Lake, which hides its own history. Beneath once existed the town of Fayerdale, a bustling economy based on iron ore, lumber and industry. Special thanks to Jack Williamson for sharing the following history of Fayerdale.

After their father's death in 1827, John Hairston and his brother George II united in partnership with Peter Hairston, their first cousin and husband of their sister Ruth, to expand the small scale iron industry begun by their father from a rich vein of magnetite in and about Stuart's Knob, a craggy hill rising five hundred feet over Goblintown Creek. The partnership was formally recorded under the name "Union Iron Works Company" (Henry County Deed Book #9, page 395). In this record, the three Hairstons agreed, "...to become co-partners together in the art or trade of manufacturing of iron in its various branches and all things thereto belonging and also in buying and selling all sorts of wares and commodities belonging to the said trade, which said co-partnership shall continue so long as majority of the partners may deem it profitable and upon the death of either one of the partners the co-partnership is not to be dissolved but to be continued by the survivors ... each put in as stock four Negro men and two Negro women slaves a piece..."

Those slaves and others dug the rich ore from shallow pits and caverns with pick and shovel, broke it by hand sledge, and carried it by ox or mule cart a quarter mile or so to the flat top of a low hill above the furnace beside Hale's Creek. They also cut great quantities of hardwood logs and stacked them in large, rounded, pyramidal piles which they set to burning and then covered with dirt to smolder several days into almost pure charcoal. With the furnace at temperature after several days of slow heating to prevent the granite structure stones from shattering, it was continuously kept "in blast" for weeks and months at a time by periodic charging with batches of mixed charcoal, iron ore, and lime stone fed into the top by hand cart as the liquid iron drained from the crucible. A large bellows driven by a water wheel at the end of a flume from above the Furnace Pond dam forced air into the burning charge to increase the combustion temperature within the crucible. The smelted liquid was run from the tap hole into molds formed in a bed of sand. The primary molds were a set of large bulbs off a common header which when filled, looked like a litter of suckling pigs, hence the name "pig iron" for the primary product of a blast furnace. On Hale's Creek, other molds were probably carved into the sand to produce crude cookware, stove tops, fire backs, plow shares, and similar wares. The cast pigs were worked by local iron smiths, including Lewis Turner whose smithy was just two miles to the west on Little Goblintown Creek, to forge gun barrels, horse shoes, wagon wheel rims, and farming tools of all sorts.

Peter Hairston died in late 1840. Shortly thereafter, John transferred his interest in the partnership to his brother, George, making George the sole owner of the Union Iron Works Company. About 1850, George obtained a 50-acre parcel known as the "Forge Tract" from Jacob Prillaman on the north side of the Smith River in Franklin County opposite the Iron Works tract in Patrick County. That facility had a small dam in the river and used water powered sledges to forge pig iron from several neighboring mines and furnaces. George enlarged the dam to increase the available water power, bought or had made the tooling required of a modern forge and smithy, and constructed the various buildings and ancillary facilities essential to the processing of pig iron. Concurrently, George's newly formed Smith's River Navigation Company was attempting to establish transport of iron and other products down river via bateau from the Forge Tract area to Martinsville.

Unfortunately, that effort failed because of the great difficulty in moving the barges back upstream, according to W.E. Trout III of the Virginia Canals and Navigations Society. None the less, after completion of facilities in about 1851, all raw pig iron from Union Iron Works was hauled to the Forge Tract by mule or ox cart over tortuous dirt and logging roads, which fortunately were mostly downhill, for processing and marketing.

Early in the 1850s, George's son, Samuel William Hairston, took over management of the Union Iron Works Company where he had built a substantial manor house. Samuel expanded and consolidated the various parcels in Patrick County associated with the Union Iron Works. In January 1862, George transferred the Forge Tract to Samuel "for affection and one dollar" (Franklin County Deed Book #27, page 106); and in June the 4,840 acre Iron Works Tract (Patrick County Deed Book #17, page 297). The following year, Samuel sold the Iron Works and Forge Tracts for $150,000 each to John P. Barksdale, Jonathan B. Stovall and Elisha Barksdale. Other than some local legends of Stuart's Knob iron being used by the Confederacy for various military uses such as girding the *CSS VIRGINIA (ex USS MERRIMAC)*, no records could be found indicating what activities occupied the settlement around the Union Iron Works from then until June 1903 when the Barksdale heirs sold the same 4,840 acres, then known as the "Iron Works at Union Furnace," to Frank Ayer Hill, Herbert Dale Lafferty, and their wives, Alice and Mary respectively, for $40,000 (Patrick County Deed Book #32, page 403).

Mr. Hill purchased several small parcels in the Goblintown area and leased 7,500 acres of John A. Hairston's former lands from Ann M. Hairston and others for the lumber thereon. In 1905, the Virginia Ore and Lumber Company was incorporated in the Commonwealth of Virginia with principals Frank A. Hill, Herbert D. Lafferty, Junius B. Fishburn, Edward I. Stone, and Thomas W. Goodwin. Later that year, the Hills and Laffertys sold their 4,840 acres, then called "Union Furnace Iron Works," to the Virginia Ore and Lumber. Hill also transferred his other interests in the area, including the 7,500-acre leasehold, to the VO&L. The area was given a new name, Fayerdale, concocted by Alice Hill from her husband's first initial, his middle name, and Herbert Lafferty's middle name.

Soon, Fayerdale blossomed into a booming mining and logging town. The mining operations in Stuart's Knob were mechanized with

41

pneumatic drills, electric lighting, iron cart railways, and a tramway -- a
powered by steam driven generators and winches in a new power
house. The confluence of Hale's and Goblintown Creeks was scooped
out to form a log storage pond serving a modern band saw mill. Twelve
miles of standard gauge rail was laid along a snaking right of way besid
Goblintown Creek and Smith River ravines to the Norfolk and Western
main line at Philpott, and stretches of three foot narrow gauge track
were run from the log pond dump ramp to cutting sites in the
surrounding forest. Other construction included a company office
building, freight station, blacksmith and carpenter shops, an ore tipple
a warehouse to handle whiskies and brandies for the DeHart Distillery
nearby Woolwine, and numerous dwelling houses, stables and other
ancillary buildings. This drawing on the next page illustrates how
Fayerdale was probably configured about 1910, the heyday of its brief
existence. The light weight logging track followed the cutting sites as
they migrated through the rapidly wasting forest.

This photo shows the impressive size of trees that were used for loggin
in the area around Philpott Lake.
(Patrick County Historical Society)

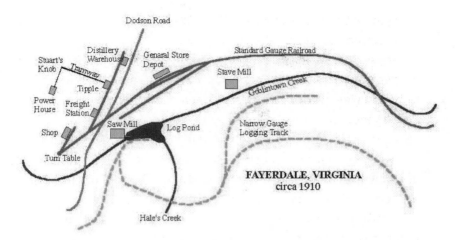

Dodson Road

Distillery
Warehouse

General Store
Depot

Standard Gauge Railroad

Stuart's
Knob

Tramway

Stave Mill

Tipple

Goblintown Creek

Power
House

Freight
Station

Shop

Saw Mill

Log Pond

Narrow Gauge
Logging Track

Turn Table

FAYERDALE, VIRGINIA
circa 1910

Hale's Creek

All of this activity was financed by a mortgage of all VO&L property, including the leasehold and rights of way, to the Southwest Virginia Trust Company of Roanoke for $300,000. In 1906, the VO&L procured, on a lease-purchase agreement, one narrow gauge (three feet) 35-ton Class B steam engine from the Climax Manufacturing Company of Corry, Pennsylvania, for $6,600, with delivery to be at Philpott by N&W Railway (Henry County Trust Deed Book #2, page 317). About the same time, the VO&L purchased outright a used standard-gauge Baldwin Consolidation 2-8-0 from the N&W. These engines were of the types shown in the following photograph.

A replica of the type of train that traveled the Fayerdale tracks.

All VO&L rolling stock was constructed at the company shops in Fayerdale using wheel sets and other parts from foundries along the New River. The standard gauge roster probably included a combination passenger/freight car, box car, flat car and several shallow gondolas. Narrow gauge cars consisted of skeleton log lorries, and one or two flat bed tool transports.

In those days, a typical train out of Fayerdale would include: a car carrying several passengers, a bag or two of US Mail, a few kegs of "stamped" legal whiskey and brandy, a half dozen barrels of dried apples or peaches, a few bushels of chestnuts, a small barrel of black walnut meats, and a barrel or two of ground tanning bark stripped from chestnut oak trees; a gondola of iron ore; and a flat car of rough cut railroad ties and other lumber. The return trip might carry, besides a few passengers, boxes and crates of merchandise for the general store, US Mail, kegs of liquor for the warehouse from stills along the Smith, and forge iron in various forms for the VO&L shops. The Climax toted lorries of workers to cutting sites in the hills about town each morning, and saw logs, strips of tanbark, and tired workers back to its home base, the log pond at the band saw mill, each evening.

The iron operation produced well, and the town continued to grow until about 1910. Then, German pig iron of equal quality to that produced from Stuart's Knob ore began arriving at the Norfolk and Western shops in Roanoke at a price equivalent to the VO&L's cost to mine the raw ore alone, before it was shipped to furnaces in Pulaski for smelting into pig. Mining operations in Fayerdale drifted to a stop, and full attention was devoted to lumbering. In 1913, the VO&L leased several thousand feet of used rail and some switch parts from the N&W to construct a turning wye straddling the general store and depot on the main line. That facilitated turning around an entire short train at once rather than just the engine and its tender on the turn table. Thereafter the end of the line turn table and run around track were removed. In January of 1916, anticipating future profitable trade in southbound lumber and northbound granite to and from Mount Airy, North Carolina, the company surveyed and took options on right of way parcels for an extension of their railroad from Fayerdale southward along the west side of Bull Mountain to Stuart, the seat of Patrick County, and on toward Mount Airy (THE ENTERPRISE, Stuart, Virginia, 3 February 1916). However, the Southern Railroad, which later merged with the N&W, strenuously objected to competition with its Danville and Western subsidiary, the "Dick and Willie," at Stuart, and with itself at Mount Airy, so the idea was dropped and the options were never exercised. With war clouds gathering in Europe, rumors of iron ore production resuming circulated in Fayerdale (THE ENTERPRISE, 19 October 1916), but those rumors never materialized.

About that time, a raging fire destroyed the band saw mill and the cut lumber stacked in the adjacent drying field. Evidently, that fire was not disastrous because the lumbering business continued to thrive in Fayerdale. During 1921, the Smith River Lumber Company, tenant at Fayerdale, advertised for, "... Saw Mill men for sawing and piling several million feet of hardwood lumber..." (THE ENTERPRISE, 17 February 1921). That level of effort hints strongly that the band saw mill and logging railway as well as the railroad to Philpott were still quite functional into at least the early 1920s. There was still lumber and farm produce to haul for profit even though the iron ore trade had ceased and Prohibition had dried up the liquor traffic. But things were not well in Fayerdale. Sporadic reports from that neighborhood published in THE ENTERPRISE in the early 1920s told of more families moving out, more feuding and shootings among the moonshining neighbors, and a general malaise in the populace. Fayerdale was dying while a few of its residents were amassing fortunes in the illicit liquor business.

In August 1925, T.W. Fugate purchased, for $50,000, all of Fayerdale's railroad and mining equipment -- including engines, rails, ties, bridges, and switches, and all mining machinery, mine rail and tools, as well as the right-of-way titles between Fayerdale and Philpott. The transaction was subject to the track and switch lease with the N&W which had been periodically extended through April 1926. Thereafter, virtually all of Fayerdale's railroad and mining equipment vanished, and the land was as before the Hills and Laffertys arrived in Goblintown hollow except for the ravished forests, abandoned rail beds, many abandoned buildings, and a few scattered relics of iron.

About the time of the Fugate transaction, Junius B. Fishburn bought out his partners in the entire former Virginia Ore and Lumber Company holdings. In 1933, Mr. Fishburn donated the then 4,868 acre known as Fayerdale to the Commonwealth of Virginia for use as a state park which he named "Fairy Stone" after the staurolite crystals shaped like tiny Saint Andrews, Roman and Maltese crosses abundant in the hills about Goblintown Creek.

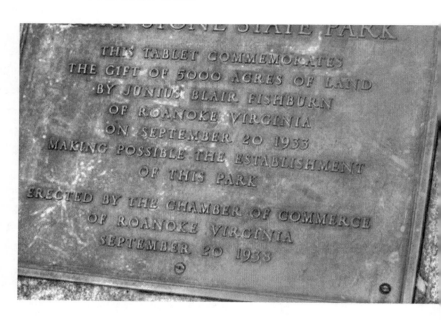

A marker at the adjacent Fairy Stone State Park acknowledges Fishburn's gift of the land. *(Nancy Bell)*

Shortly thereafter, two companies of the Civilian Conservation Corps set up camp at the foot of Stuart's Knob in the vicinity of the old ore tipple and began grading access roads along the old lumber trails. In the course of their work transforming the area, they seriously disrupted what had become Fayerdale's principal industry, moonshining. But the CCC also provided many customers for that not so clandestine business in their squads of young workers. By 1936, those workers had completely razed Fayerdale and dammed Goblintown Creek. Before flooding the hollow, they relocated their camp to higher ground a half mile or so to the north and east, and levelled the original site to lay in a new section of the main road to Dodson and Union Bridge, Virginia State Route 623, above the flood line. By their departure in the spring of 1941, the CCC crews had adjusted the hilly terrain to provide paved roads, a sandy beach, picnic areas, camp sites, bridle paths and walking trails. They built a bath house, restaurant, and cabins for visitors as well as a water and sanitation system.

Several barred entrances still mark areas of access to iron mining operations like this one at Goblintown Creek. *(Nancy Bell)*

3

NATIONAL
MARBLE MILLS
ATLANTA, GA.

Customer's Acknowledgment
7/25/16

Mr. Quince Haynes,
Elamsville, Va.

Ship to Fayerdale, Va.

Die   0.6 x 0.4 x 1.8
Base   0.8 x 0.6 x 0.3
B.B.   1.0 x 0.10 x 0.6

> **IMPORTANT.**
> If we have not correctly entered your order, kindly return this acknowledgment AT ONCE with proper corrections.

Son Willie Haynes
June 28 1901
Dec 29 1917

"Christ loved him and took him home"

Clasped hands in place of emblem.

Examine shipment at depot carefully, and if there is any damage, have agent note such damage on the freight bill before accepting the shipment.

Design No. 3000-D	**Material** White	**Order No.** 5861
Ship Sept 16	**With Nos.** Same time as Nos. 5860	

File No. 385   **Price** $23.10

If Correct
O K Here

Sold by

Mr. E. C. Hall,
Dodson, Va.

Ronnie Haynes of Patrick County provided this receipt for headstone engraving from 1916, when Fayerdale was a thriving town.

FORM 30

No. 116   Fayerdale, Va., 3/14 191 2

Received of _____

By _____ Self

Gross Weight, 1455 Lbs.

Wagon Weight, 750 Lbs.

Net Weight, 705 Lbs.   Bark

VIRGINIA ORE AND LUMBER CO.

By _____ Clerk

This 1912 receipt for milling was made by the Virginia Ore & Lumber Company.

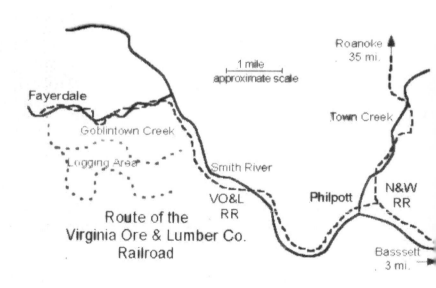

(Jack Williamson)

Hazel Hale's scrapbooks tell the stories of the people who once lived under today's Philpott Lake. In one series of photos, a man called Grover is seen with two arms, one arm (after getting the other arm caught in a belt at the mill) and no arms (after a hunting accident took the remaining arm). Yet Grover was said to have saved a child from drowning and often drove a manual transmission truck. Despite his disabilities, he continued to earn a living by having other people be the hands of his work while he instructed on topics of several skilled trades.

51

Beauice + Loy Carter

1918
Tol Menders, Rena Carter Menders
Sol Ingram,
Clemence Custer Ingram,
Rose + Clemence are children of
Johnnie + Nedlie Law Carter

L-R:
Mr. Colonel Graham
Mr Grover Custer
(was written on back of original picture)

Ralph Carter...born 1913

Lindsey Carter and good
family friend, Hazel Jones
Webb.....for whom Hazel
Via was named

Back-L-R:
Raymond Carter,
Paul Carter holding .....
.
Hazel Via
Lessie Carter Via holding Ada Via,
Nellie Via seated center left
Front-L-R: Ellen Carter
Bernice Carter
Ann Via

Rosie Carter

Grover Carter

L-R:
Ida Martin Carter ?

Louise Bryant M.Villia
(Loey's mother)
Loey being all the Car
children;
Martha Carter
Raymond Carter
;

52

Miller's Granddaughter is Keeper of Lake History

Jamison Mill was a three-story gristmill built by Flem Jamison in the late 1880s. It operated until it was flooded as part of the reservoir project, around 1950. Hazel Via Hale, now in her 80s, is the granddaughter of Robert Carter, the miller at Jamison Mill for over 50 years. "It was a gathering place for the whole community," she said. "People came for miles to have corn ground into meal and also to visit for a while."

Hazel Via Hale is the official keeper of history of the Jamison Mill area of Philpott Lake. Although reluctant to claim the title, Hale, 82 years old in 2015, turned her written recollections into a book *Memories: Jamison Mill Era*. The book is self-published and sells for $10 a copy.

The home Hale shares with her husband, Roy, is filled with scrap books containing sepia toned and black-and-white photographs of life around Jamison Mill before the community was permanently flooded to create the reservoir at Philpott Lake. She began creating the books as a teenager and continues creating them to this day. As she flips through the dog-eared pages recalling the past, Hale narrates the fascinating stories of the people who lived there, of the mill and of the time when folks were forced to higher ground. With ease, she identifies each face in every photograph held in the keepsake books by white pasted-on corner tabs.

Most of it is from memory although much effort has been put into writing with silver pen on black pages the names and dates of people and occasions. Ask about a person from the area, and Hale probably has a photo of him. Her books are rich with people on horseback, family gatherings, children playing and stern-looking families posing for posterity.

Recently, Hale herself was photographed sitting near the old hearth made of native stones on the property of her grandfather's family home. She and Roy return to the old "Carter" home site to clear brush and visit flowers planted by her grandmother that yet bloom in the dappled light. Most of the yard is underwater, but the knob where the house stood contains traces of the family who once lived there – building materials and garden remnants. On the next hillside reside similar artifacts from a family (also named Carter but unrelated) who lived there when Hale was a child. She remembers playing with the children, who would meet in the middle for games of ball, tag or hide-and-seek.

The mill itself was not just for people to bring corn and wheat for grinding, Hale said. It was a place to meet socially. Fish fries, corn shuckings and horseshoe games were held. A feature the children called "the sand hole" was a place for them to play together, Hale recalls. A nearby summertime favorite was a cave-like swimming hole where the water had cut into the bank, and swimmers jumped from a large rock overhead. Another spot, "Spruce Pine Hole" featured large rocks and deep water for jumping in.

As the women visited, they quilted or canned fruits and vegetables or prepared meals for visitors or after-church socials. Other gatherings were not so wholesome, Hale noted. The men gathered to play cards and relax after a hard week in the fields, at sawmills or working out of town. Moonshine was often consumed, and fights broke out from time to time. Mostly, there was telling of tall tales, catching up with one another, sharing Depression-era struggles, and watching the children play.

For a better idea of where Jamison Mill was located, Hale refer to a place located on what was Nicholas Creek in Franklin County near the village of Henry (formerly known as Alumine). The mill was surrounded by hills and stood a quarter of a mile from where the creek emptied into the Smith River near the Patrick County line. Hale remembers from childhood visits to the mill that a gigantic belt around a large pulley system worked the mill's turbine under the mill floor. "This caused the entire building to vibrate," she said. "It was a deafening roar." The terrain was so rugged that customers without oxen

54

used ground sleds or hoisted sacks on their backs for transporting by foot -- "some actually did this on stilts to cross the creek."

Jamison Mill neighbors came together to watch as their town vanished under water, Hale said. "The dam was completed in 1952, but by January 1953 water had already partially covered the mill site. By fall of 1953, the reservoir was filled to capacity and Jamison Mill was completely under water." Jamison Mill Park was created in the 1960s, and Hale was an inaugural member of "Friends of Jamison Mill Park," a group which continues to keep the park free of litter and debris – to build trails and to host family-centered activities reminiscent of the "good old days."

Hazel Hale learned in 2010 that work on the trail at Jamison Mill Park would come very near to the family home once occupied by the miller. She and her husband, Roy, got permission in 2011 to bring in their own tools and clear the area around the remains of her grandfather's home. It is located on a hill overlooking Philpott Lake that formerly overlooked the mill. A chimney of mud and stones is all that remains of the homestead today, and it is only a few yards away from water's edge. Standing inside the rubble that was the heart of the home, Hazel points to a washtub her grandmother once used for flowers and reminisces about days gone by. The sloping "yard" with daffodils planted long ago in early bloom, dips down to the lake. Forsythia bushes planted by Hale's grandmother flourish along the shore. The rusty remains of an old stove, a car bumper and other tubs litter what was the side yard. Evidence of a former roadbed in front of the home site remains. Across the cove is a clearing that once held another Carter family's home – the Johnny Carter place. Because of the elevation of the home sites, neither Carter family ever fell victim to flood waters from Nicholas Creek.

About a month after the Hale's visit to the homestead in 2011, a portion of Nicholas Creek escaped its banks at the Jamison Mill Park entrance snatching away anything in its path. The Hales stood on the shore and watched the roiling brown water with white caps journey on its way. One can only imagine what they were thinking.

Hazel and her husband, Roy, visited the homestead at Jamison Mill to clean the area where the family home once stood. Inset: Ancestors pos for an early photo in front of the house that once stood on the hill.
(Hazel Hale)

Hazel Hale sits on what once was her family's hearth. *(Hazel Hale)*

Roy Hale watches as Nicholas Creek threatens to wash away a popular hiking trail at Jamison Mill Park. *(Hazel Hale)*

8-4 Franklin News-Post,Rocky Mount,Va.,Thurs.,Nov. 29, 1973

Drives without Arms

G. W. Carter of Route 1, Henry, has spent the last 65 of his 66 years without arms. But that hasn't prevented him from working as a plumber and electrician, nor has it stopped him from driving his truck (above) or lighting cigarettes or writing. The Franklin County native has eight children, 17 grandchildren and six great-grandchildren.

Jamison Mill, circa 1950, was built in the late 1880s. Pictured are the children of Wilson and Mamie Carter Prillaman: Curtis, Doris, and Lowe Prillaman. These are the grandchildren of Bob and Lucy Carter, who operated the mill. *(Hazel Hale)*

Flood Catches Local Woman's Father, Others

"We never knew where he went -- not until Murphy Smith told us he'd found the body." --Louise Mabry

When Louise Cooper Rorrer Mabry was eight years old, her father, Noah Cooper, left their home near the Smith River and did not return. Several weeks later his body was found miles downstream. The shoes still tied around his neck told the story of a man trying to cross a flooded stream and getting caught in the sudden rush of water making its way down from the mountains and into the low lands.

Before the late 1940s, flash floods were a way of life in and around the community known as Philpott near Bassett, Virginia. The Smith River was an unpredictable presence known to swell out of its banks without much notice taking property, animals and sometimes people with it. The many creeks dotted along the Smith were not immune from such flooding. Mabry recalls the fear that would arise within her when the sound of rushing water upstream could be heard because it meant that lots of water was coming fast, and its path was unpredictable. Noah Cooper was 50 years old when he drowned in what was once called Branch Creek near Prillaman Switch.

While sad, Mabry's story is not uncommon. The infamous Flood of 1937, which stole her father's life and the lives of several unconfirmed others, also caused 1,500 people in the region to be evacuated from their homes and resulted in more than $600,000 in damages -- a huge amount for that time in history.

Mabry, now in her 80s, was forced to move several times after 1937 as the Philpott project progressed. The first move was to where the dam is now – to the Helm House in the vicinity of the old iron bridge that linked Bassett to Fayerdale. While at the Helm House, she remembers her grandfather being jolted around in a horse drawn buggy that transported him to medical care across the bumpy railroad ties. Later, planks were laid across the railroad bridge to enable people to

59

cross on foot, on horseback or by carriage in safety and relative comfort. The bridge is now underwater, she said.

Mabry and her brother (George) and mother (Becky Shelton Cooper) moved a lot after her father's death, sometimes living in boarding houses or with relatives. They were relocated several times t escape the reservoir filling up, eventually settling at Brown Hill. "It was hard way to grow up. We really struggled to survive," she said.

"I was late going to school. It was so far to walk," Mabry said. The first school she attended with any regularity was Republican Schoc at Brown Hill. Mabry describes it as a one-room mountain top school. Attendance depended on the weather, the harvest and other factors that superseded school at that time in history.

Mabry's grandfather, Pete Shelton, fathered 12 children as wa the norm in the secluded mountains of Virginia in the 1920s and 30s. Family gatherings were large, and the families did without luxuries.

"The people weren't happy to move when the reservoir was being built," Mabry recalls. "They were close-knit, and didn't want to live too far from one another." Mabry took time to draw a map of the area before the lake was made, noting railroad tracks that are now underwater, homes, churches and stores.

"Now they are all scattered," she said.

About 30 families were displaced to make way for Philpott Lak Some of the homes were left to be covered by water. Others were destroyed before the water began to rise. As the population began to thin, Postmistress Nannie Rosabell "Rosa" Barnes noted that only a few of the former patrons came in to the postal office that she managed at Philpott station. Construction workers from all over the country frequented her post office, however during the building of Philpott dar She is quoted as saying that "the mail came in from all over" during tha time because of all of the out-of-state constructors on the job. Barnes survived all the changes living to the ripe old age of 101, long past the time the store and post office finally closed.

The sons of Bob and Lucy Mullins Carter are left to right, Grover William Carter (May 11, 1907-March 27, 1977) and Harry Clifford Carter (April 20, 1905-September 29, 1923). Grover lost his right arm to a belt in the mill and his left when he dropped a loaded gun over a fence while hunting. *(Hazel Hale)*

61

Louise Mabry at about the time of her father's drowning in Nicholas Creek. *(Louise Mabry)*

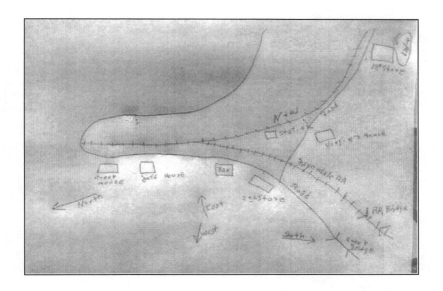

Mabry recalls her childhood in Fayerdale with a drawing indicating where friends, family and neighbors once lived.

Pete and Louise Shelton with Bulah and Minnie. *(Louise Mabry)*

Louise Mabry *(Nancy Bell)*

Joe Yeaman recalls days of wilderness before the dam. *(Nancy Bell)*

Surveyor Recalls Wildness of the Area before Construction, Interactions with the People

In his role as Survey Party Chief for J. A. Gustin & Associates, Joe Yeaman of Patrick County has seen Philpott from a unique perspective. His crew surveyed about 21 miles of the area running clockwise from the bridge at what is now Ryan's Branch public boat landing. Before the US Army Corps of Engineers began the work of building the dam and creating the reservoir, many creeks and mountain features in the area served as landmarks -- Runnett Bag, the Calico Rock, Puppy Creek and White Falls, for example.

Yeaman recalls how the area was so wild that the survey crew would spend several hours getting to where they had left off the previous day. Despite renting a 4-wheel drive vehicle, some days required two-hour hikes in and out of the area. "You just didn't go where we went," he said.

Yeaman and other professionals working on the project respected the people who lived there. "We would stop at the little stores and gathering places along the way to let the word out about what we were doing and where we would be going," he said. This was as much a measure for the workers' safety as it was a courtesy to the people who lived there, he noted. Many of the creeks along the Smith were famous for bootleg liquor operations, and interlopers could risk their lives if mistaken for "revenuers" or rival moonshiners. Crossing private property was part of the job, and the surveyors and the moonshiners shared a common goal of staying out of one another's way. At the time, other dangers included sheer cliff faces, snakes and a variety of wild animals, said Yeaman.

A somewhat later and more sinister recollection of Yeaman's is the kidnapping of the police chief of nearby Eden, North Carolina. Although he was shot through several times and left for dead at the "old #1 ramp," the chief survived. More recently, a missing woman's remains were found in an oil drum at the bottom of the lake near Ryan's Branch,

Yeaman said. While searching for a weapon in another case, police found the barrel and solved the murder mystery.

Then there was the moving of graves to higher ground to mak way for the reservoir. In March 1951, RR Herndon of Smithville, Tennessee, began work for cemetery relocation, completing the work two months later. Yeaman's uncles helped move the graves, he said. One of the cemeteries that remain today is Shady Rest Cemetery.

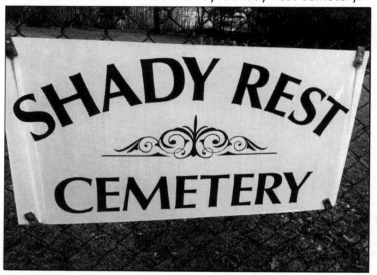

The entrance to Shady Rest Cemetery (Nancy Bell)

Trudging through a thick carpet of freshly fallen autumn leave at Shady Rest in Bassett, Yeaman points out the relocated graves – all shaped the same and bearing the name of the deceased person. Most of the markers, however, indicate that remains were never identified. Others bear the names of families who once lived in Fayerdale, the town beneath the lakes. Some even memorialize the remains of Nativ American ancestors who remained in the area through the 1940s. All show evidence of the passing of time: mosses, tarnished nameplates and a bit of landscaping neglect.

"The history of the area is fascinating," said Yeaman. Now retired, Yeaman lives in Patrick County and continues to explore and discover as much about the history around Philpott Lake as he can. Survey maps he shared were donated to the Bassett Historical Center and also to this project. They can be accessed at the West Piedmont Planning District Commission mapping office in Martinsville.

A blanket of leaves covers the ground where markers of those whose remains were moved from below Philpott Lake were relocated.

Names on the markers of the relocated remains are hard to read as the copper plates are green with tarnish.

THE MILLER and HIS FAMILY LIVE THROUGH THE GREAT DEPRESSION

Local mills were a necessity for the people of the hilly terrain around what is now Philpott Lake. Farmers brought their own grain and received in return previously ground meal or flour, minus a percentage, which paid the miller. On occasion, they were paid in currency, but more often in goods. Most towns and villages had their own mill so that local farmers could easily transport their grain there to be milled. The people of these communities were dependent on their local mill as store-bought bread was a luxury few could afford.

Bob Carter was Jamison Mill's last miller, a job he held for 50 years. People traveled throughout the area to bring corn and wheat for grinding. It was dangerous work, and one of the miller's sons, Grover, lost an arm to the milling process when it was caught in the belt that turned the grindstone. The unfortunate Grover later lost the other arm in a hunting accident. Still, he is said to have driven about the county leaning his chest on the steering wheel. Using his left arm stub, he later rescued a child from drowning by pushing up from the bottom and grabbing the child with his legs.

Unable to find employment due to his handicap, Grover manufactured moonshine to feed his growing family. He was jailed for two years after being caught, but later bounced back, teaching others skills like fishing, plumbing and electrical work by having his "students" serve as "his hands" for his odd jobs. Others became caught up in the making and distribution of illegal liquors as a way to support their families. The area's rich history of moonshining is well documented, and the resulting violence between rival moonshiners did much to drive many families from the communities around Philpott Lake before the reservoir project even began.

Depression times also made people more resourceful as the miller's granddaughter related in her history of the Carter family. Before the reservoir was built, the miller and his wife, Lucy Mullins Carter, actually made an abandoned school, the former High View School, home for themselves and their eight children. The home was without electricity or running water. In addition to milling, Carter ran a store a[nd] a blacksmith shop out of the same complex. His business sense includ[ed] constructing the occasional temporary cane mill for making molasses. To accomplish this, a horse walked a pole attached to two drums around a ring until the cane stalks were crushed producing syrup. The miller also raised bees and had a clubfoot for which he designed a special brace, according to his granddaughter, Hazel Via Hale, of Henr[y] Virginia.

Life as a mill family during the economic depression of the 1930s was tough, according to *Memories: Jamison Mill Era*, Hale's boo[k] about the Carter family. Rainwater was caught in barrels for washing clothes. Scrubbing boards and wooden or metal tubs were items of Depression-era Jamison Mill. Clothes were boiled in heavy iron pots over fires. This required constant stirring to prevent scorching, a very physical job. After rinsing in clean water, clothes were dropped into a tub and then wrung by hand. They were hung out to dry on clothesline[s,] fences, or over bushes. Ironing was not any easier. Irons were made h[ot] on coals from the fire, soot wiped off, and potholders used to protect hands from the heat.

From her mother, Hale learned that the Carter's tiny front roo[m] was used for "courting," and couples often fought one another off for the chance to sit by the fire in that room. In the winter, water often froze over Nicholas Creek, and people rode horses over it using ice nai[ls] on the horseshoes to keep them from slipping. People cut large chunk[s] of ice for their icehouses and kept them for summer months. Accordin[g] to Hale's mother, heating the school house-turned-family home was difficult. Lined plank walls were covered with newspapers and cardboard to help keep winter winds out. The children broadened thei[r] vocabularies by reading this "wall paper," Hale said.

Dangers of the time included rabies, flash floods, influenza an[d] extreme poverty. Stories from the late 1930s and early 1940s describe people developing rabies after exposure to sick animals. People stayed very aware of the water level at Nicholas Creek and the Smith River. Flash floods often resulted from heavy rains or thunderstorms upstream. The Carter family lost an 18-month-old to drowning.

They were not immune to the flu epidemic which overspread the area during World War I. Hale relates that while most coffins in the vicinity were made by Kemper James of Ferrum, the locals made their own when they had to. For the homemade caskets, the women made a lining of sheet cloth from the general store. Men crafted the coffins of wood with silver colored latches.

The Carters were families who lived in and around Philpott for many years. The children of one Carter clan who lived on a hill near Nichola Creek often joined another clan from an adjacent hill in the low area below for play. *(Hazel Hale)*

Growing Up in a School House:
Carter Descendants Recall a Tough but Happy Life

Ed Johnson remembers the old schoolhouse that the Carter family made their home. Johnson married Bob and Lucy Carter's daughter Martha in 1938 and visited the home often in the 40 years that the family lived there before the lake swallowed much of the yard.

Johnson recalls "courting" Martha and, due to the distance traveled and rough terrain, being allowed to stay overnight at the Carter home occasionally. "I slept upstairs. In the morning, Martha would sneak up there and wake me up with a little kiss," he remembers. "I thought that kiss must be the sweetest kiss that any girl had ever given a boy." If Mr. Carter had ever learned of those kisses, Johnson said there would have been big trouble. "You just didn't go around kissing each other before you were married in those days."

Mrs. Carter, Johnson remembers, baked the best chocolate cakes around and often entertained preachers on Sunday afternoons. Legend was that she could "take a burn out" – meaning that she could make a burn stop hurting. How she did it remains a secret even now. Later, married to Martha, Ed and their children lived with the Carter family for a while just a few years before the family was forced to relocate. Grandpa Bob would get on the floor and play with the children, Johnson said. "He would chase the kids and make a pinching claw with this hand," Johnson said. "He would say 'Old Bloody Bones is gonna yet ya' and the kids would scream and laugh…. Sometimes they would get scared."

His wife, Martha, recalls many cold winters growing up in the old schoolhouse. Snow often blew in between boards, and the children slept with their heads under quilts. In the morning, they would shake the snow off the quilt. The family's large 4-feet long by 4-feet wide fireplace was inefficient and could burn up to a truckload of wood on a cold day. When Martha returned as a married adult with her own children, Ed asked if the fireplace could be blocked up and a heater installed. Bob Carter agreed, but Lucy, the matriarch, (who was wearing two pairs of socks, long johns under her dress, a sweater and a coat in the house) replied: "I don't like that idea narry a bit." Despite her objections, Ed Johnson and Bob Carter traveled to Rocky Mount where they purchased a heater for $3.

"We went home, and I put a piece of tin over the fireplace, cut hole for the stovepipe, and hooked up the heater," Ed recalls. I those days heaters were oiled in the factory to keep them from rusting. "We started the fire and that oil had to burn off. It filled the house with smoke, and I had to open the doors to get all the smoke out." Fortunately, Grandma Lucy was not in the house at the time. By the time she arrived, the house was smoke free and warm. "Then she looked at me with a crooked little grin and said 'I am sure sorry. I just didn't know it would be warm like this!'" The fireplace remained closed for as long as the house stood.--*Recorded in a note to Hazel Via Hale from Ed Johnson*

Historians and Residents Gather in 2013 to Remember Life before Philpott and Fairy Stone Lakes

Presentations about Fayerdale and Philpott Lake are popular among people who grew up around the lakes. In 2013, they gathered in the Fayerdale Hall on the Fairy Stone Park campus, to share their recollections.

John McGhee grew up in Bassett in the area around Horseshoe Point. His great-great grandfather purchased the land in 1858, but he was killed at Petersburg in the Civil War. McGhee's Grandmother (Jarrett Family) grew up on Goblintown Creek and married and had land across the Creek. They had large farms of 350-400 acres each. They were happy and made a living from farming. The reservoir project "was not welcomed," McGhee said. "This was not a gift from the US government. It was a battle." Horseshoe Point was named for its shape and was very isolated. To go to Rocky Mount or Martinsville you had to take the train from Goblintown to Philpott and switch trains.

Joe Philpott's parents ran the stave mill from 1914-1916. Staves are wooden slats used in barrel making. The family moved out of Fayerdale when the children were young. He and his family lived near the train tracks at Philpott station in a white clapboard house that still exists. Philpott remembers a Cincinnati traveler who came often, he said, for the cooking. "But it was really for dad's corn liquor." Philpott remembers that a Henry County Sheriff once came in on the train to investigate "a killing" in Fayerdale. "He said 'I'm not going there by myself.' " Philpott's dad went with the sheriff. They rode mules into moonshine territory.

Charlie Philpott says he has been going up and down the river for 82 years. He remembers that some people lived in homes where the cracks between the boards offered a view of outdoors and the weather. "They had it pretty rough." In 1999, a drought reduced the water level so low at Philpott Lake that an island was visible that usually is under the lake. He knew of one family who had to cross the Smith in a boat twice a day to go and come home from school at Horseshoe Point.

Joe Hollandsworth, 83, fell from Philpott Dam during construction. He was raised below the dam, and recalls the flooding that took place before the dam was built. When he was 14, he worked beside one of the men charged with killing moonshiner Ewell Cox, just out of prison. Cox was infamous for his role in a liquor-related shootout in Fayerdale. Hollandsworth's mother-in-law told him she witnessed a shooting in Fayerdale in the late 1920s. The man fell over a barrel after being shot in the chest.

Kenney Kirkman is a renowned railroad historian. He said Patrick County once had three narrow-gauge railroad lines that were used for hauling lumber. "They would cut tree branches, throw them down, lay rails out, cut timber and then move the rails to the next timber site," he said. The journey from Fayerdale to Philpott took 2 hours when the train was full. "If you left the windows open you were likely to get scratched by briars and branches coming in." In 1999 during a drought Kirkman walked the old rail bed and picked up railroad spikes and other items. He saw bricks, flowers blooming, foundations of old homes, and Indian arrowheads, now all under water once again. Kirkman added that Fayerdale was once considered as the site for Ferrum College because of its proximity to the railroad. "We could have had a college here instead of a lake," he mused.

Linda Burnette Fain worked as a waitress at Fairy Stone Park restaurant from 1970-76. She collected photos from folks who lived in or near Fayerdale. Fain created a video of the photos and stories she heard from visitors of the restaurant. The CD is for sale at the Fairy Stone State Park visitor center and is widely used to reconstruct the history of the area.

Coy Young, a Bassett barber, is said to be the keeper of hundreds of stories told to him by people in the area during visits to his shop in the many years he has been the area's favorite barber.

Rudy Johnson was born in 1935 and moved to Salt House Branch in 1945 to care for a grandparent. He only stayed 3 years, because in 1948, they were displaced by the building of the dam and the rising water. "We had no running water, no electricity, and I walked three miles to catch the bus as a kid," Johnson shared. The dam was "traumatic to my grandmother, Maud Lovell. I think it led to her early demise. She never signed any papers or agreed to let them take her property." Maud Lovell died before her property was sold to the government for $4,000. When Johnson's dad was 14 years old, he would walk from Salt House Branch to the train and would travel the rails to cook at the lumber camp. "They had pinto beans and cornbread every day for breakfast and lunch," he said.

Doug Stegall collects Fayerdale and other historical objects from the area. His father "chased bootleggers all over the county." Stegall owns a Civil War era whiskey flask. Fayerdale was the hub of DeHart Distillery. Mountain Rose (now a Patrick County Inn) was the family home of the DeHarts. At one time, the family had distilleries in Philpott and Woolwine. When Prohibition was eminent, one of the DeHart brothers encouraged people to buy a 10-year supply of his "medicine." Legal whiskey went out the front door. Bootleg out the back, he recalled.

Above, the lawn at Fairy Stone State Park overlooks a lake that cover the former town of Fayerdale. Below, the store and post office at Philpott Station near Bassett Mirror Company was recently torn dow

Philpott Lake: What is in a Name?

When it came time to name the lake created by damming the Smith River near Bassett, Philpott was the logical choice. The Philpotts, a clan of lumber cutters, saw millers, preachers, merchants, farmers and politicians, held properties throughout the area. In fact, 406.5 acres were purchased from the Philpott family for the reservoir project. The town of Philpott, which is located at the back of today's towering dam, was founded by Albert Buchanan Philpott in 1905. Albert married Mary Elizabeth Farner Helms Philpott and they had seven children, ensuring that the Philpott name was a permanent fixture in the area, where Philpotts continue to live today. In the 1900s, the town had two general stores, a barrel stave mill, a railroad station, and a railway that extended to iron mines and legal distilleries in Fayerdale, the once upon a town located under Fairy Stone Lake.

The town's founder opened a general store in Philpott in 1905 after the Virginia Ore and Lumber Company erected a narrow-gauge railroad from Philpott to Fayerdale, a community also swallowed by water and now referred to as Fairy Stone Park. In connection with his business in Philpott, he carried on extensive saw milling activities and operated the general store in Philpott until 1916, except for the two-year term (1914-1915) he served in the Virginia Assembly as a delegate from Henry County.

In Richmond, A.B. Philpott made a name of himself as an accomplished and versatile member of the House of Delegates. "A preacher, manufacturer, merchant, farmer and statesman, he is clever in each department, combining the best features of the varied assortment of callings and rounding out into the whole the characteristics that go to make a real man and a genuine progressive," said an undated article in a Richmond newspaper. "While not known for his talking, Mr. Philpott sometimes takes the floor, but it is usually when called upon by the speaker to open the session with prayer. His voice has excellent carrying qualities and can easily be heard over all the hall of the House of Delegates."

During the time he was in the Assembly, Philpott's daughter, Rose Williams, ran the store at Philpott. Rose was later appointed postmistress of Bassett. After A.B.'s death, the store and lumber business was taken over by his three sons: Edward Jefferson Philpott, John E. Philpott and Charles Thomas Philpott. The business grew and prospered through the years as a general store, but primarily as a lumber business.

Descendants of Albert Buchanan Philpott & Mary Elizabeth Helms Philpott Recall Rich Family History

Patrice Philpott Newnam is the official history keeper for the Philpott family. Using her knowledge of technology, she has built a website, where the many descendants of the Philpott family can go and keep family history alive with photos, stories, memories, events and genealogy.

Her mom, Jo Anne Garland Philpott, is a champion of historic preservation in the town of Bassett where an old train depot has been converted to farmer's market spaces in large part due to her efforts. Much work remains to be done and, although in her 80s, Jo Anne continues to work to return it to the bustling center of activity again along the abandoned streets of a crumbling factory town. The beautiful natural environment of her adopted hometown is also important to Jo Anne. She supports efforts to keep the Smith River clean and the verdant wooded areas around it pristine and to share the area with others via interpretive trails. She is a fixture at Bassett Historical Center and Martinsville's courthouse museum – all preserving history of the people and place that surround her precious Philpott.

Charlie Philpott, Jo Anne's husband and Patrice's father, delivered groceries in the area surrounding Philpott as a boy. He did farm work and watched as the boys went off to war by boarding the train at Philpott station and riding north to Roanoke for points overseas.

John Philpott, who ran a store next to the post office, said the Philpott Dam construction workers did not buy much. "Those new ones don't buy anything but a few groceries. The folks up the valley wanted farm machinery and equipment, fertilizer, seeds and this was the only store from here to Fayerdale, 12 miles up. Now those people are scattered everywhere, and the new ones don't make up the difference," he is quoted as saying in a Martinsville Bulletin account of the project.

Charlie Mize held onto his prize farmland until forced to move. His wife had said they would live there until they died. An unnamed old woman is quoted as saying that she would stay in her home until the water came up to her front door – and then she'd go out back. She hu on until 1949, when her family came from Roanoke to retrieve her.

One holdout family was Johanna Stone (66) and her son. They lived in the bottom land 3-4 miles upstream of the dam and about a mile from the river. The government was late in buying her land because of some ownership dispute that later was cleared up. She had lived there 21 years and was uncertain where she would go.

"It has gotten right lonesome since they closed this road down below the dam though. People used to pass here all the time, but now you never see a soul," she said in the final days in her home.

Jo Anne Philpott and her daughter, Patrice Newnam. *(Nancy Bell)*

THIS APPLICATION must be filed with the Clerk of the Corporation Court of Your City or Circuit Court of Your County

FORM NO. 7

APPLICATION of a widow of a soldier, Sailor, or Marine of the late Confederacy under act approved March 26, 1922, as amended by acts approved 1926, 1930, 1932 and 1934.

I, _Mary H. Philpott_ do hereby apply for a pension under the provisions of the acts of the General Assembly of Virginia relating to Confederate pensions.

I do solemnly swear that I am a citizen of the State of Virginia and that I have been an actual resident of the said State for one year next preceding the date of this application, and that I am the widow of _____ who was a soldier (sailor or marine) in the service of the Confederate States in the War Between the States, and that I was married to him (See note below) and to the best of my knowledge and belief during the said war my husband was loyal and true to his duty, and never at any time deserted his command or voluntarily abandoned his post of duty in the said service, and that I was never divorced from my said husband, and that I never voluntarily abandoned him during his life but remained his lawful wife up to the time of his death, and that I am a widow at the date of making this application, and that I am now entitled to receive a pension under the provisions of said act. I do further swear that I do not hold a

national, State or county office, which pays a salary or fees exceeding one thousand dollars ($1,000.00) per annum, nor have I income from any and all sources whatever exceeding one thousand dollars ($1,000.00) per annum nor do I own in my own right, nor is there held in trust for my own benefit, estate or property, either real, personal or mixed in fee or for life, which yields a total income exceeding one thousand dollars ($1,000.00) per annum. I do further swear that I do not receive a pension from this or any other State. I do solemnly swear that the answers given to the questions which I am required to answer in this application are true to the best of my knowledge and belief.

Any assessment of property does not affect the right to pension, but the gross income from all sources must not exceed $1,000.00 per year. Certificates under B, C, D, not necessary if husband was pensioner.

NOTE.—Widows seventy-five years old or over can receive pension regardless of date of marriage. Widows under seventy-five years old are required to have been married prior to January 1st 1921.

1. What is your name? _Mrs Mary H. Philpott_
2. What is your age? _84_
3. Where were you born _Huntva, Va. Henry County_
4. How long have you resided in Virginia? _All life_
5. How long have you resided in the City or County of your present residence? _All life_ years.
6. Where do you reside? If in a city, give street address. Post office _Bassett,_
   County of _Henry_ Virginia
7. With whom do you reside? _Daughter Miss Annie Philpott_
8. What was your husband's full name? _William Garner Philpott_
9. When, where and by whom were you married?
   When? _Nov 20, 1870_
   Where? _Fruntys, Virginia_
   By Whom? _Rev. Garna Lee_
10. When and where did your husband die? _At home Bassett, Va. 2ND Oct 21, 1936_
11. What was the cause of his death? _Old Age_
12. Have you married since the death of your husband? If yes, give full particulars? _No—_
13. Are you a Widow now? _Yes—_
14. In what branch of the army did your husband serve?
    _____ Regiment.
    _____ Company.

15. Who were his immediate superior officers?
    Colonel _____
    Captain _____
16. Give the name and address of a comrade who served in the same command with your husband during the war if living. (Not necessary if your husband was a pensioner.)
    Name _____
    Address _____
17. Name source of income, and what income have you from all sources? _Have no income—_
18. Was your husband on the pension roll of Virginia? If yes, in what county or city was his pension allowed? _Bassett, Va. Henry County_ ✓
19. Have you ever applied for a pension in Virginia before? If yes, why are you not drawing one at this time? _No—_
20. Is there a camp of Confederate Veterans in your city or county? _No—_
21. Give here any other information you may possess relating to the service of your husband which will support the justice of your claim. _____

A signature made by X mark is not valid unless attested by a witness.

WITNESS _____

Mary H. Philpott
Signature of Applicant

I, _J. D. Dillon_ a _Notary Public_ in and for the _County_ of _Henry_ in the State of Virginia, do certify that the applicant whose name is signed to the foregoing application personally appeared before me in my _County_ aforesaid, having the aforesaid application read to her and fully explained, as well as the statements and answers therein made, and the said applicant made oath before me that the said statements and answers are true.

Given under our hand this _6_ day of _October_ 19'6 _D.D.A. Dillon_

An application for widow's benefits after the loss of a husband in 1835.
(Charles and Jo Anne Philpott)

This stock certificate for $50, is from a time when Philpott Lake was a bustling center of activity for locals and a popular tourist attraction.
(Charles and Jo Anne Philpott)

Rosa Barnes, Philpott Postmistress. *(Martinsville Bulletin)*

Charlie Philpott celebrating the Fourth of July in the Philpott parade
(Charles and Jo Anne Philpott)

Sue Philpott Wade, mother of George Wade, waits with a cage of chickens at the Philpott train depot, which are on their way to Roanoke. Below, a hunting party assembles near Philpott.
(Charles and Jo Anne Philpott)

A wheat "thrashing" begins. Locals gathered to help cut and stack whe
on large poles for drying. Below, Jo Anne Philpott fishing at the lake th
bears her name. *(Charles and Jo Anne Philpott)*

Philpott Project: Timeline At-a-Glance

Supplied by Charles & Jo Anne Philpott

- **1934** – Philpott Project appears as part of House of Representatives comprehensive plan for the development of the Roanoke River and its tributaries – a project that was deemed "economically unjustifiable."

- **1937** – Historic flood causes extensive damage to industrial, commercial and residential properties along the Smith River in Bassett (VA), Philpott and surrounding areas of Franklin, Henry and Patrick counties.

- **From 1938 – 1946**, six proposed alternate development plans are produced each with varying: locations for the dam, type of dam, location of powerhouse, and location of the spillway.

- 1946 – Meeting of the Federal Power Commission and Corps of Engineers determines that a *concrete gravity dam*[1] with a powerhouse at the *toe* [2] of the dam was more economical than the alternatives.

- **1946-47** – Contracts are awarded to Ralph E. Mills and Sprague & Henwood for subsurface investigation at the dam and possible quarry sites in the vicinity of the dam.

- **1948** – The RW Mitchell Company of Winchester wins the contract to construct an access highway from Route 57 west of Bassett to a point near the Franklin County end of the proposed dam. Included in the contract is the construction of the approach loop and parking areas at the end of the access highway, site of the current day overlook at Philpott Park.

- **1949** – Contracts for furnishing of sluice gates[3], penstocks[4], stop logs[5], generators, hydraulic turbines[6], frames and guides, intake gates[7] and other equipment for the dam and powerhouse are awarded.

---

[1] A **gravity dam** is a massive sized dam fabricated from concrete or stone masonry. They are designed to hold back large volumes of water. By using these materials, the weight of the dam alone is able to resist the horizontal pressure of water pushing against it. Gravity dams are designed so that every dam section is stable, independent of any other dam section

[2] **Toe of the dam** is the junction of the downstream face with the ground surface.

- **February 1949** – M.F. Mason of Bassett begins construction of an engineer's office, allied buildings and other facilities, finishing the work in July.

- **June – December 1949** – W.E. Graham & Sons of Cleveland (NC) constructs an addition to the access highway from the existing road to point on the right bank of the river near the proposed dam.

- **July 1949** – A team made from the Bates & Rogers Corporation of Chicago (IL), Morrison-Knudsen Company of New York (NY), and Peter Kiewit Son's Company of Omaha (NE) bid lowest for the contract to construct the dam. Bates & Rogers supply the supervisory personnel for much of the work.

- **August 1949** – Preparatory work – installing the cableway, construction the mixing plant and building storage facilities, is started in the middle of the month.

- **October 1949** – Construction of the cofferdam for Stage 1 river diversion begins. Excavation inside the cofferdam continues until February 1950.

- **March 1950** – Concrete is first placed in monoliths. There are 28.

- **April and May 1950** – Sluice gates are installed. **May 1950 – August 1950** – Concrete is placed in 11 of the 20 apron blocks. Six of 10 section

---

3The **sluiceway** is an opening at a low level from a reservoir generally use for emptying or for scouring sediment and sometimes for irrigation releases.

[4] A **penstock** is a sluice or gate or intake structure that controls water flow or an enclosed pipe that delivers water to hydro turbines and sewerage systems. It is a term that has been inherited from the earlier technology of mill ponds and watermills.

[5] **Stop logs** are large logs or timber or steel beams placed on top of each other with their ends held in guides on each side of a channel or conduit providing a temporary closure versus a permanent bulkhead gate.

[6] **Hydraulic Turbines** transfer the energy from a flowing fluid to a rotating shaft. Turbine itself means a thing, which rotates or spins.

[7] The **intake gate** is a device in which a leaf or member is moved across the waterway from an external position to control or stop flow.

of the training walls alongside the apron or stilling basin also are completed. Work during this period is affected by heavy rains. On May 30, the Smith River breaks through the downstream end of the cofferdam and inundated the excavated area for the apron. The contractor's crane and several pumps are lost to the rising water. g

- **August 1950** – Despite the setback caused by flooding, construction of the upstream cofferdam for State II river diversion begins.

- **September 1950** – A flash flood forces contractors to flood the area between the upstream and downstream via a break in the downstream cofferdam. Although the cofferdam developed several leaks, it did not breach. The flood poured about 12 feet of water through the opening.

- **October 1950** – Installation of first penstock section is made. Penstocks are installed through January of 1951. **January 1951** – A fire develops in the cableway operation house. The system is inoperable due to fire damage until March 1951.

- **February 1951** – Bulkhead[8] and sluiceway installed in monolith 12 along with the 5' pipe used in Stage III river diversion.

- **March 1951** – Line drilling is resumed on the apron area, and three contractors for (1) cemetery relocation, (2) drilling/grouting, and (3) alterations to Fairy Stone State Park's dam begin work.

- **May 1951** – RR Herndon of Smithville (TN) completes cemetery relocations. Volunteer Construction Company began clearing the reservoir.

- **Second Quarter 1951** – Philpott Lake begins to fill creating a total storage capacity of 250,000 acre-feet and a surface area of about 4 square miles with 100 miles of pristine shoreline.

- **April 1952** – Rock excavation in the apron[9] area begins. Dam is 86% complete.

---

[8] A **bulkhead** is a retaining wall used as a form of coastal management, akin to a seawall, or as a structural device such as a partition.
[9] The **apron** is a platform below a dam or in a sluiceway along a shoreline to prevent erosion.

When all was completed, construction of the dam required 110,000 cubic yards of excavation, 26,000 lineal feet of drilling, 320,00 cubic yards of concrete, 265,000 barrels of cement, and 610,000 tons of crushed stone and sand for aggregate – final cost $6.5 million.

The powerhouse at Philpott Dam was constructed of reinforce concrete, structural steel framework covered brick, glass block and cas building stone. JA Jones Construction Co. of Charlotte (NC) constructed the facility for $1.2 million.

Three turbines were furnished by James Leffel & Co of Springfield (OH). These turbines are served by two 9' diameter and on 3' diameter penstocks furnished by Gary Steel Products of Norfolk (VA.

General Electric Company provided the generators; Westinghouse Electric supplied the main control board, station contro panel, switchgear, and allied equipment.

The penstock of the Philpott Dam is put into place.
(US Army Corps of Engineers Collection)

Early work includes blasting away part of an adjacent hill and building a
coffer dam to redirect the flow of the mighty Smith River.
(US Army Corps of Engineers Collection)

The work was at least twice disrupted by flood waters.
(US Army Corps of Engineers Collection)

An early photograph of the hillside as it is prepared to hug the first monoliths. *(US Army Corps of Engineers Collection)*

In the distance, a bridge over the Smith is erected to enable construction of the dam. *(US Army Corps of Engineers Collection)*

The cylinder is used for holding concrete, which was hoisted onto a
cable and maneuvered over the dam building site as needed.
(US Army Corps of Engineers Collection)

Workmen traveled from North Carolina and various parts of Virginia to
complete the dam building project.
(US Army Corps of Engineers Collection)

Above, steel reinforces the monoliths in preparation for pouring of concrete. Below, concrete is dumped from a cylinder maneuvered by an overhead cableway. *(US Army Corps of Engineers Collection)*

The massive dam-building operation also included construction of a number of roads and bridges, including this one at Ryan's Branch. *(US Amy Corps of Engineers Collection)*

Construction of Philpott Dam took several years and workers employin a variety of trades. *(US Army Corps of Engineers Collection)*

The hillside across the Smith River from where the current Philpott Lake Visitor Center now stands withstood blasting to prepare it for the first monoliths to be constructed. *(US Army Corps of Engineers Collection)*

This bridge was used to get construction equipment and crew from one side of the Smith River to the other.
(US Army Corps of Engineers Collection)

The dam begins to take shape, while once quiet country roads are frequently traveled by construction equipment and workers.
(US Army Corps of Engineers Collection)

A cable system transports concrete and rock from a quarry construction just for the Philpott project near today's Bassett Mirror Company. *(US Army Corps of Engineers Collection)*

Lumber frames will support concrete at the base of the dam. *(US Army Corps of Engineers Collection)*

The cable system used to position components of the dam and for pouring concrete is seen in these two views of early construction. Not how the bedrock below has been blasted into a shape that will firmly hold the dam. *(US Army Corps of Engineers Collection)*

Bedrock is blasted away in preparation for forming the first cement supports. *(US Army Corps of Engineers Collection)*

In the earliest photos of the dam as it rises from the floor of the Smith River, debris is seen floating at the baseline. *(James Kirk West Collection)* Below, pulley system used during construction. *(US Army Corps of Engineers Collection)*

A sign at the site of the Philpott Dam building project displays details about the scope of the project. Next page: Looking from the hill where today a viewing platform exists, excavation of the area is evident. Water will cover the area within one year of the excavation.
(William Ramsey Collection)

The area is completely cleared to make way for the reservoir. Below, the reservoir begins to fill. Soon the treetops will be completely under water. *(William Ramsey Collection)*

A view of the reservoir being formed as seen from today's overlook at the Philpott Lake Visitor's Center. *(William Ramsey Collection)* Below, the same area with the water higher. *(James Kirk West Collection)*

During work on the dam, a quarry was constructed near where Bassett Mirror stands today. Many tons of gravel were needed to complete the project. *(US Army Corps of Engineers Collection)*

Early into the project, the Smith River is diverted away from the site where the first monoliths will be constructed.
(William Ramsey Collection)

This aerial view of the construction site shows the Smith River still in place. The circular road on the top of the hill overlooking the river is now the site of a visitor center and park.
(US Army Corps of Engineers Collection)

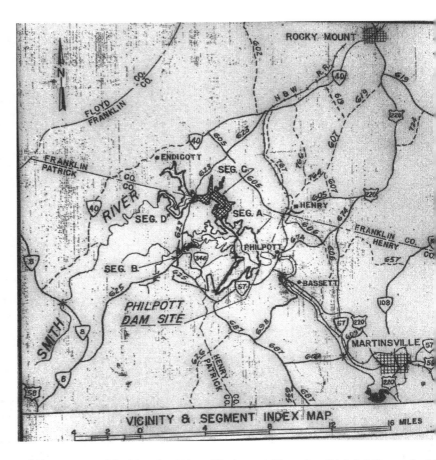

This map provided by the West Piedmont Planning District Commission shows the Philpott Dam site in relation to the three counties it intersects.

CCC Makes Reservoir Building Possible at Nearby Fairy Stone Lake

The Great Depression of the 1930s brought a storm of hunger and almost unimaginable hardship to millions of Americans, but with dark clouds there were silver linings to be seen in the form of the CCC and its projects at what is now Fairy Stone State Park adjacent to Philpott Lake.

If you were a member of the Civilian Conservation Corps (CCC) at the time Fairy Stone Lake was created, you would be awakened each morning at 6 a.m. by a whistle-blowing camp leader signaling the beginning of a new day. You would roll out of your tightly spaced bunk, hit the floor and assemble for morning roll call and the daily raising of the American flag. You would race back to your bunkhouse to make your bed, wash up and put on denim work clothes. By 7 a.m., you would march into the mess hall for breakfast followed by an inspection of the bunkhouse much like those required in the US Armed Forces. By 8 a.m., you and twenty-nine of your peers would assemble into one of many work crews. As you boarded a truck for the job site, you would reach for the brown paper bag that held the same lunch every day: 1 bologna sandwich, 1 peanut butter-and-jam sandwich, and a piece of fruit.

At 6 p.m., you would again assemble around the American flag as it was put away for the night. You would go to your assigned table for dinner. From 7:30 – 9 p.m., you might visit the Post Exchange where soda, candy and other treats could be bought with merchandise coupons. The amount of coupons used would be deducted from your monthly pay of $30 -- $8 of which you could keep and $22 that would be sent back home to family.

The CCC was President Franklin D. Roosevelt's answer to the devastating unemployment of the Great Depression and existed between 1933 and 1942. A half million young men were paid $30 a month to build roads, dig ditches and to work on other infrastructure improvements, like the Blue Ridge Parkway, Fairy Stone Lake locally, and throughout the US as well.

The work at Fairy Stone included road building, creation of trails, installing a beach, and constructing bathhouses, a concession building and log cabins. Between 1933 and 1941, more than 3 million young men served in the CCC.

"Its contributions in Virginia were significant: 15.2 million trees planted for reforestation and erosion control, 986 bridges constructed fire hazards reduced in over 152,000 acres, 2,218 miles of new telephone line strung, and 1.3 million fish stocked into various lakes al streams. The conservationists also worked on the restoration of historical sites at Jamestown, Williamsburg, Yorktown, Fredericksburg and Spotsylvania and combated floods along the James and Potomac Rivers."

To understand more about the multiple roles the CCC played in th communities in which they served, these excerpts are from the December 1, 1939 CCC newsletter called "1389 Speaks." The newspap was published twice a month by the "Journalism and Mimeographing classes of the University of Fairy Stone..."

"In answer to a hurry call from the town of Stuart, every available man from Company 1389 spent the week of November 13-18 fighting forest fire. The blaze started on the powder dry slopes of Bull Mountai north of Stuart and Patrick Springs and burned over 20 square miles of forest. The Stuart water supply was threatened, and three homes were destroyed. During the week an average of 96 men from 1389 were on the fire line daily. They constructed over 20 miles of fire line in some of the roughest and most inaccessible country in Patrick County."

"Until the latter part of August, Company 1389 held the district safety flag. Our camp was the leader over all other camps in the Southern District in consecutive months without a lost-time accident. Then, an epidemic of accidents occurred. A broken thighbone in the quarry, a shortened finger in the workshop started it. Since August, we have had an accident almost every month. This week a wild swing with an axe almost resulted in injury."

112

PART THREE
The Moonshine Economy

Franklin County has been called the Moonshine Capital of the World – mostly for the volume and variety of spirits produced and the longevity of the trade, which has been traced back to the late 1700s. Many raids took place near where Philpott Lake's Johnny's Ridge is located.

Shooting Creek, Runnett Bag Creek and other vertical mountain areas provided hiding places with abundant water sources for liquor making. In 1935, a large sting operation identified law enforcement officials who were in on the money-making opportunity that illegal liquor sales provided.

Between 1930 and 1935, 37 tons of yeast, 16,920 tons of sugar and thousands of tons of malt, meal and other ingredients of moonshine making were said to have entered the county. In the early 1970s, one of the largest operations was busted. It contained 20 719-gallon vats and was located off Prillaman Switch Road between Ferrum and Henry followed by a similar yield from an operation in Ferrum later the same year.

What follows is one man's front seat view of the trade in the area around Philpott Lake.

Morris Stephenson and his dog, Victor. *(Nancy Bell)*

Newsman Documents Decades of Illegal Liquor Making

When Morris Stephenson left his hometown of Marion (VA) to work with his mentor "Red" Kermit Salyer at *The Franklin News Post*, he had no idea the move would submerge him in the world of illegal liquor making – so quickly or so completely.

Stephenson, who hails from a "newspaper" family, was in Rocky Mount less than a week when called upon to cover the first of many raids on illegal stills in Franklin County (the self-appointed Moonshine Capital of the World) for the *Post* and a now defunct sister newspaper. Since then, he has covered dozens of raids, written a book on the subject, and consulted with a television crew on a reality show.

"That first story was hilarious," Stephenson admits. "I basically wrote what the agents told me. It's a stupid story – embarrassing."

Years of reporting have made him an expert of the subject. As the only active reporter at the *Post* in the early 1960s, Stephenson was dispatched to every raid on moonshine makers to document with his words what he learned and with his photos what he witnessed. Often, that was more than one raid per week!

It was quite a coup for a cub reporter, but a happy coincidence got him the first story and kept the stories coming until the newspaper publisher finally told him to stop covering all the raids on stills unless they were really big because "the front pages of the newspaper were all starting to look alike."

What was the coincidence that gave Stephenson such insight into distilling and selling moonshine? The night of the first raid, Stephenson struck up a conversation with one of the ABC (Alcohol, Beverage Control) agents learning that the man hailed from his own hometown. The agent took the young reporter under his wing providing unprecedented access to raids from then on.

"The first camera I used was one of those 4 x 5 cameras with the wooden frames that had to be switched out between shots," he said. As cameras evolved, he always had one in the car and a multitude

115

of rolls of film at the ready. He has honed the craft in such a way that his photos are much admired. Stephenson's photos have appeared in publications, historical collections and adorn the walls in poster-sized canvas of the newly minted Bootleggers' Café in Rocky Mount.

He has come to be known as an expert on the topic of moonshine making, the people who make the moonshine, the equipment, and wh makes the best (and the worst) "shine."

One of the largest raids attended by Stephenson was an 800 gallon still featuring 36 "mash boxes." In the late 1960s, distillers discovered a more efficient way to manufacture whiskey without all th mash boxes, and he was there to witness the very change in production.

"Quality of liquor has gone way down," Stephenson shared. "The process has been cheated by making it quicker by pumping it full of sugar."

The original way to make moonshine included no added sugar at all, he said. Corn was soaked in a creek and laid out on a dry cloth to sprout. Then it was ground to make "pure corn whiskey," Stephenson explained. "Submarine-type" stills are the ones most frequently used i Franklin County, although some "shiners" have been known to use car radiators to process whiskey.

"They boiled them out first," said Stephenson, quashing the rumor that drinkers often got sick of lead poisoning. "It's just not true Agents have taken samples of every still raided here, and not one had lead."

Some of the most memorable raids took place in recent years according to Stephenson. One, which took place in the community of Penhook in 1993, stands out in Stephenson's mind because productio took place in a metal building right on the shore of Smith Mountain Lake. Another, in the mountainous community of Providence, feature a "fake" cemetery that looked real from the air where ABC agents are known to look for moonshining operations. Below, however, were fak headstones and a real pathway leading to a building thought to be pa of a cemetery, but really used for whiskey making. In 1999, Operation

Lightning Strike resulted in indictments for 30 people and the arrest of Ralph Hale who ran the Helms Farm Exchange out of a storefront ironically situated next door to the sheriff's office and courthouse in Rocky Mount. His operation was said to have produced more than 210,000 gallons of moonshine between 1992 and 1999.

The cat and mouse game played out by moonshiners and ABC agents continues today. Timber man, Cecil Love, was said to make the best apple brandy in the county. ABC agents busted the Fork Mountain resident in June of 2011. Despite the fact that 55 barrels were "ready to run," Love was eventually released from custody and avoided charges due to a technicality.

"Cecil had never been charged with anything – had not even had a speeding ticket," said Stephenson. "He was never caught making or hauling. He earned a Purple Heart. He's a good guy."

After years of asking his contacts to allow him to observe the liquor-making process, Stephenson was granted the opportunity in the 1980s. Arriving under the veil of night, he assisted with the making, learning through hard work the craft. This night of making liquor is detailed in his book, *A Night of Makin' Likker and Other Stories from the Moonshine Capital of the World,* which is available on Amazon.com

Most recently, Stephenson served as a consultant on the reality television show "The Moonshiners," where his expertise was put to the test by the rowdy and popular "Tickle" and friend Tim Smith of the show. Stephenson added the two celebrity whiskey makers to the list of contacts he has made over time. Occasionally, he touches base with them.

A non-drinker these days, Stephenson said he is still up for a taste of what is being made in the region from time to time by swishing it around in his mouth but not drinking it down. Admittedly, there are not that many shines that can be tolerated any length of time without burning the mouth.

"Franklin County's been good to me," said the 79-year-old Stephenson who sports an Energizer Bunny pin on his shirt pocket. The icon reminds him of the pacemaker that keeps his heart ticking and his reporter's instincts strong. With occasional raids on illegal distilleries throughout the community still making news, he needs to be ready for the next big story.

A group of "shiners" poses at their secluded mountain still place.

DeHart Family Well Known for Distilling Spirits

The name DeHart is synonymous with liquor making in the early 1900s in Patrick and Franklin Counties. Family Patriarch, Fleming DeHart, born in Patrick County in 1838, had a thriving farming business along with one that produced legal whiskey. Fleming's two sons eventually took over management of the business, creating the Fleming DeHart Distillery Company at the turn of the century. The distillery shipped liquor to many parts of the country, primarily by rail.

When the brothers decided to bottle the whiskey for ease of transport, older brother, Ike DeHart, had labels designed using variations of the family name, like "Old Ike." As their fortune accumulated, the younger DeHart brother, Joseph, did not feel he was getting a fair share of the profits, so he started a distillery of his own, which he called Mountain Rose Distillery. It was established near Woolwine (VA). The brothers used their labels to take jabs at one another as seen in Joseph DeHart's turn-of-the century statement: "I have not made up a dozen or more names for my whiskey and as many prices…" He proclaimed his "plain and simple corn whiskey" more reliable than his older brother's brand. Additionally, Joseph sold his for 50-cents a bottle cheaper than his brother's, which sold for $2.50 per bottle. Prohibition changed the business of whiskey making and selling forever.

A 1916 advertisement circulated in the Philpott area by the Mountain Rose Distillery advised: "Make Hay While the Sun Shines," and urged consumers to purchase as much liquor "as you can" before the November 1 coming of prohibition. The ad was titled "Preparedness," and it stated that after November 1 of 1916, "You will not have the privilege of fortifying your home with pure 100-proof Mountain Rose Corn Whiskey, made and sold strictly on its merits; nothing purer or better for medicinal purposes…" Noting that good whiskey will be hard to find, the text urged the consumer, "It would be no bad idea to lay away a ten years' supply of CORN WHISKEY… and you will never regret it."

The illegal making of liquor became a cottage industry in the years that followed, especially during the Great Depression when other sources of income were scarce. Homemade stills were crafted. Corn whiskey was produced, and jugs of the illegal brew were sold locally and to northern and western cities, creating steady income for families who otherwise would have very little or none. It is said that during the Depression, and even afterwards, lawmen often turned a blind eye to illegal whiskey-making knowing that its production was putting food on the tables of very poor people. The area continues to be referred to as the "moonshine capital of the world," for the quantity of product produced along the streams of the Smith River.

Getting the whiskey to customers included cat-and-mouse games between moonshiners, rivals and "revenuers," characterized by speeding cars, gravel back roads, and head lamps off to avoid detection. It is said that the popular sport, NASCAR, evolved from efforts of moonshiners to outrun these agents with their cars. The business of distilling illegal whiskey became a violent one with loss of life from shoot-outs involving rival whiskey makers as well as revenuers. Revenuers were employees of the Internal Revenue Service who were charged by the federal government to prevent illegal production and distribution of alcohol during the period of Prohibition in the US. Nellie Shelton, in a 1966 interview with Park Receptionist Peggy Pinkerton, recounted her memories of Fayerdale's illegal liquor making. Shelton said almost everyone was involved and that violence resulted when one moonshiner reported a competitor to revenuers. Elmer Haynes wrote a book about a series of moonshine related murders called "The Fayerdale Tragedy."

The counties surrounding Philpott Lake, particularly Franklin County, continue to be a source of illegal liquor making to this day. At least twice a year, newspaper articles describe raids on modern-day stills.

Corn whiskey labels, like this one from the DeHart's, are considered works of art.

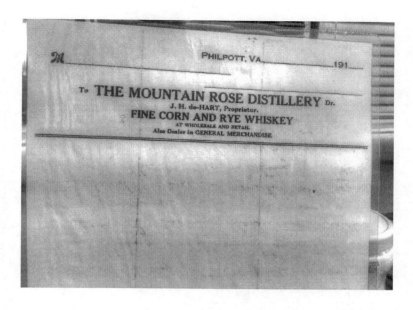

An early invoice from the Mountain Rose Distillery, one of the DeHart's holdings in the early 1900s. Instructions below, were located on the back of the distillery form and are for a craftsman to construct a cold water reservoir for making whiskey. *(Charles and Jo Anne Philpott)*

Build a small resovoir at Spring to keep out mud & frogs, then bring water from this one to a second resovoir down the branch far enough to get in a resovoir the height & size I wish to build for storage. The pipe connecting the two resovoirs should be under ground so as to keep water supply cool.

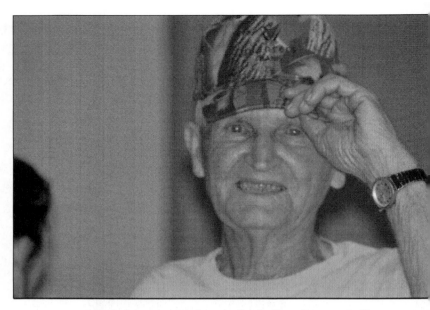

BK Hodges tips his hat at the ladies. *(Nancy Bell)*

Flatfooting and Moonshining Way of Life for Hodges

Flatfooting is a type of folk dance in which the dancer's footwear is used musically by striking the heel, the toe, or both against a floor or each other to create audible percussive rhythms, usually to the downbeat with the heel keeping the rhythm. As the dance has evolved over the years, many localities have made contributions by adding local steps and rhythms to the style. The dance has origins in Wales and England. In the fifteenth century, the all-wooden clog (clogging) was replaced by a leather-topped shoe with a one-piece wooden bottom. By the 16th century a more conventional leather shoe with separate wooden pieces on the heel and toe called "flats" became popular, from where the terms "heel and toe" and "flat footing" derive.

Orphaned as a young man, BK Hodges (now in his 80s) scrambled to make a living the best way he could. In the mountains near Ferrum more than 50 years ago, liquor making proved most lucrative, he said. His experiments at making corn whiskey were successful. Within a few years, he partnered up with a competitor and a lifelong business was born.

I met BK by coincidence at a Crooked Road musical performance in an International Harvester dealership turned music hall. Outgoing by nature, BK was busy flatfooting his way around the room, greeting members of the audience, engaging the band, and trying to encourage nearly every woman in the room to join him on the dance floor. When he began talking to me, I was not sure whether he was being honest or telling tall tales, but a few conversations with others later, it was obvious he is something of an icon around Ferrum, Rocky Mount and Ridgeway where his distilling abilities are legendary.

With his trademark toothpick jutting out, Hodges explained that he had many "still places" over the years. Moving operations from place to place helped him elude law enforcement and keep his record clean.

He parlayed his earnings into owning several gas stations in his prime, and generally had a good life, he said.

Except for one accident while making moonshine that left his torso and upper thighs badly scalded. "I was in the hospital for a right good time," he said. When his doctor left for a scheduled vacation, BK checked himself out and went home to Ferrum.

"I had this white pair of pants, and I cut big holes in 'em where the burns were," he said. Taping bandages to the pants was a lot more comfortable than taping it to the skin where removal was bound to be painful. During a string of days – he does not remember how many, BK sat under a shade tree with the bandages off so that the wounds could dry naturally.

"When the doctor got back, he didn't know how those burns had got healed so fast..." He was amazed. I explained about the book in progress and he agreed to share a few details of his moonshining operations.

"The really good money was made from hauling," said Hodges. For years, using a half-ton truck, he delivered moonshine up the Eastern Seaboard.

"We'd stop in Richmond. That fella would take what he wanted and we would head to Washington. He'd get what he wanted, and we'd go on to New York." Hodges said, "It was a lot of driving, but also a lot of money made that way."

As he danced around the music hall, eventually taking off his characteristic red jacket, BK tipped his camouflage hat at the ladies, smiled for pictures and stopped now and then to just appreciate the experience, folks cheered him on.

Something of a legend at the annual Galax Fiddler's Convention, he kept in shape by flatfooting to his favorite old-time mountain bands – those that employ washboards, worn fiddles and big basses.

As the music stopped and the crowd started thinning, BK danced over to my table. "You gonna put me in the book?" he asked. When I nodded affirmatively, he said as if thinking twice about it, "You know I ain't never been caught."

PART FOUR
Keepers of the Lake – US Army Corps of Engineers Maintains the Dam, Ensures Safety

The US Army Corps of Engineers at Philpott Lake is responsible for the safety and daily operations of the dam that created Philpott Lake, along with educating the community about the lake and its many parks and ensuring that the area remains pristine.

US Corps of Engineers staff after a meeting about the area before Fairy Stone Philpott lakes were formed. Below, Philpott near the site of the Philpott family home, Bassett Mirror (where Indian artifact excavation took place), and former Philpott train depot. *(Nancy Bell)*

Craig Rockwell provides a tour of the Philpott Lake Visitor Center, her with his beloved Philpott Lake in the background. *(Nancy Bell)*

Rockwell Says Philpott is about Natural Beauty, Economic Development

The Lord is my shepherd, I shall not want. He maketh me lie down in green pastures. He leadeth me beside the still waters. He restoreth my soul. – Craig Rockwell (Personal Mission Statement Psalm 23:1-2)

Craig "Rocky" Rockwell will be the first to tell you he only intended to stay in Bassett for about two years. The avid history buff from Wisconsin worked in Colorado and other areas of the country for most of his career. He came east to become Operations Project Manager at Philpott Lake as a last stop before retirement. He has been here since 2009 and finds it difficult as he enters year six to talk about leaving. As he has come to appreciate the natural beauty of the place, Philpott Lake has become near and dear to his heart.

"This is one of the most pristine lakes in America," he notes with pride. "We have forests and wildlife and lots of clean water." Early in his time at Philpott, budget cuts could have forced at least one of the parks surrounding Philpott Lake to close. Rockwell refused to let that happen.

"Which park will you close?" Rockwell was asked. "Not one," he answered incredulously. "We will keep them all open and even more visitors will come," he remembers answering.

Friends of Philpott was founded to provide volunteer support of the parks – as a way to help keep some costs down but also to provide opportunities for locals to appreciate their parks and help ensure they stayed open. The very active group blazed trails, hosted clean-up events and sold firewood to stay in business. They were joined by folks outside the area who had visited Philpott and wanted to help preserve it. In summer, the out-of-town volunteers stay tucked back into long-term camping spaces and spend their days helping where needed.

Park visitation has increased annually in Rockwell's tenure, despite a recession and threats of additional budget cuts. Infrastructure improvements include a handicapped accessible playground and restrooms at Bowen's Creek Park, a regulation sized dock for tournament fishing, restroom upgrades -- a marina.

Still, he appreciates the need to balance preservation of the natural environment that makes Philpott so special with the need to stimulate visitation to the area and contribute to the tax base in a meaningful way.

"When jobs leave and unemployment increases it's easy just t look at the bad," says Rockwell. "But we have worked very hard to position Philpott Lake as part of the economic recovery of the region. Bringing visitors from outside the area is one very significant way to d this."

In addition to partnering with Henry County on the marina project, Franklin County helped fund a regulation fishing pier which ha brought hundreds of thousands of dollars into the region by enabling the lake to be the site of tournament fishing, Rockwell says. The economic value of every visitor to Philpott Lake is presently $28.27, Rockwell explains. The park gets upwards of 650,000 visitors each yea and that number increases annually as park features are added.

The economic impact goes beyond tourism, however. "We're providing about $7 million annually in flood control," and electricity so back to the power grid produces income each year as well. The value c land protected from flooding by the dam at Philpott is three-quarters a billion dollars, he explains. This is not a figure Rockwell tosses about casually but based on a number of factors like land values, acreage an potential loss of property, and a complicated mathematical algorithm.

"While recreation is certainly a large part of what Philpott has to offer, the dam creating the lake was built first and foremost to protect the community below," says Rockwell. Authorized as one of tl first Water Resource Development Act areas, the project was on the federal government's radar as early as the 1920s and came to the forefront after a devastating flood in 1937 nearly washed away the town of Bassett. The Flood Control Act of 1941 eventually included construction of the dam on the Smith River that would create Philpott Lake.

Flooding was a way of life for the people of Bassett, Stanleytown, Fieldale, Philpott and even Collinsville and Martinsville before the Philpott Dam was completed around 1950. A severe thunderstorm in Floyd County, for example, could cause sudden and devastating flooding downstream without a drop of rain ever falling on the hills around Philpott. Taken unaware, the people would not have time to prepare for the onslaught of water. Lives, livestock and property losses were a regular part of life before the dam was built creating Philpott Lake. Historical accounts tell of people running for trees to escape roaring streams -- of toddlers being swept into the water as it raced by -- of homes being swept off foundations in the night with only the sound of rushing water upstream as an often "too late" warning.

Convincing most people to abandon the low ground that now rests at the lake bottom was not difficult for those who had seen the tragic consequences of flooding. Others hung on until the water started rising around their porches and they were forced to walk out with their possessions held high above them. Once the dam was built and the reservoir filled, however, a greater appreciation developed – especially during the 1960s through 1980s when visitation to Philpott Lake peaked and Coast Guard boats patrolled to enforce safety regulations amid the crowds of swimmers, boaters, sunbathers and skiers.

By the late 90s, with the implementation of the North American Free Trade Act (NAFTA), visitation had fallen as the furniture and textile industries around the lake closed and nearly 10,000 people lost jobs. The pristine lakes were quiet and the woods grew thick around them. For locals, Rockwell says, Philpott Lake became one of the best kept secrets around: quiet, a great place to fish and hunt.

"But 'best kept secret' really isn't a good business model," said Rockwell. To that end, the Corps has been working for the past decade to increase visitation to the lake in a way that does not overly impact the natural setting. Philpott Lake has more than 3,000 acres of shoreline. That which has not been developed into a park is mostly

131

forest, right to the water's edge. So when a new "county owned" marina was added in 2014, it included only the basics – some boat slip gasoline pumps and a place to purchase convenience items, like fishin lures. This was done deliberately to preserve the rural nature of the lake, says Rockwell.

This is but one example of how the US Army Corps of Enginee staff that Rockwell supervises has reached out to the community in unprecedented ways. Others include historical lectures, environmenta expos, family-centered events and friends groups for the lake's many parks.

"So we really have four missions: flood protection, hydroelectric power generation, recreation and environmental stewardship," Rockwell explains.

A unique partnership Rockwell says is the one the US Army Corps has with Dan River Basin Association (DRBA), a regional nonprof organization with an environmental mission statement and coordinatc of this project.

"I don't know of any other partnership like that which we hav with DRBA," says Rockwell. DRBA "gets the concept that promoting ar protecting go hand in hand," he says. We believe it is possible to prote the natural beauty of the place and also to bring in more visitors without upsetting the delicate ecological balance. "In the end, it's abo quality of life, and they get it."

Park Ranger Shares the Philpott Story

"Those who don't know history are doomed to repeat it."
— Edmund Burke

It was the wheel of a railroad car at the Fairy Stone Lake visitor center that first sparked Dan LaPrad's interest in the once bustling town of Fayerdale. LaPrad, a member of the US Army Corps of Engineers staff at Philpott Lake, became fascinated with the stories of the railway that once existed under Fairy Stone Lake and set out to learn as much as he could about the abandoned town below.

One of the first sources LaPrad found was Jack Williamson's internet article about the iron works, lumber and milling operations that operated there, in a place called Fayerdale, prior to the 1930s. http://www.angelfire.com/folk/goblintown_mill/Fayerdale/Fayerdale.html. Fayerdale was a place of steep mountains, low valleys and earth rich with veins of magnetite in and about Stuart's Knob. At one time, slaves used shovels and ox drawn carts to remove the mineral for smelting and timber could not be cut fast enough to fuel the fires of the furnace that processed the material. A railroad was built to haul goods out and supplies in. During the Civil War, iron from the area was used to produce artillery. The area prospered.

Prosperity was not to last. Pig iron imported from Germany was less expensive than what was produced at Fayerdale. As the US began to buy iron from Germany, production at Fayerdale completely stopped. Demand for lumber for the smelting furnaces left the area logged out, so timber sales were not an option. Fayerdale fell on hard times as The Great Depression hit. Living in the area became a daily struggle. The mountainous terrain created a barrier to traditional farming and isolated the people from jobs in nearby towns. Eventually, some families began to make and sell liquor. Legal distilleries sprang up, and product was shipped out of the area by rail. Prohibition came, and it had violent consequences for the people of Fayerdale. Tales of shootouts between rival moonshiners -- of wounded men staggering from the woods and falling dead -- and other ghastly stories drove many residents out of Fayerdale way in advance of the time when the land was flooded to create a lake.

LaPrad has pieced together a detailed history of life at Fayerd. with help from Williamson and others who have come forward with stories, photos and memorabilia. His history goes something like this....Small scale iron mining began in the 1800s on a hill rising five hundred feet over what was once called Goblintown Creek where an opening to the mine remains today. Goblintown, sometimes called Bo Bottom, is so named because of the many animal bones found there from a former Indian settlement. The Union Iron Works Company produced pig iron from a blast furnace. Local ironsmiths forged gun barrels, horseshoes, wagon wheel rims, and farming tools. In 1905, th Virginia Ore and Lumber Company was incorporated, and the area wa given the name, "Fayerdale," a combination of the owners' names. A company office building, freight station, blacksmith and carpenter shops, a warehouse, and numerous dwelling houses sprang up arounc rail line that was primarily used to haul goods in and out, but also to ferry passengers.

Junius B. Fishburn, later a managing partner in the Roanoke Times & World News (Roanoke VA) bought out his partners in the Virginia Ore and Lumber Company holdings in the 1930s, and he donated the then 4,868 acres known as Fayerdale to the Commonwealth of Virginia for use as a state park. That park was a project of the Civilian Conservation Corps (CCC). It was later named "Fairy Stone Park" for the many staurolite crystals shaped like tiny crosses found even today in the hills about Goblintown. By the spring 1941, the CCC crews had constructed paved roads, a sandy beach, pic areas, campsites, bridle paths and walking trails. They built a bathhou restaurant, and cabins for visitors as well as water and sanitation systems.

LaPrad is now something on an expert on the history of Fayerdale having given more than a dozen presentations on the topic. LaPrad's research paints a vivid tale of what life was like, learning as he goes from people who attend presentations and offer new tidbits of information. He is the first to admit that his role of late is to become something more like moderator, as people attend who can add new knowledge to what is known about the ill-fated town.

One product of the work is a Google Earth® map that he and his boss, Craig Rockwell, have assembled. The map is populated by homes and mills and stores and other features recalled by those to have provided recollections for the project. The interactive map provides a virtual tour of Fayerdale and the surrounding area prior to the development of both Fairy Stone and Philpott Lakes. It will continue to be updated as new information is added.

While LaPrad says he will continue to give the presentations "as long as people will come," his hope is that some younger people will continue the work.

"I think a lot of what Fayerdale has to tell applies to today," he says. The Fayerdale economy crumbled in part due to Germany providing cheaper iron ore than could be produced at home. Today, the area suffers from foreign competition that has gutted the local furniture and textile industries, he noted.

"Those who don't know history are doomed to repeat it. I think there is a lesson there," LaPrad said.

Dan LaPrad spends part of his time sharing the history of Philpott and Fairy Stone Lakes. (Nancy Bell)

Yesterday's Features, Today

Philpott Lake was an immediate favorite place for locals to enjoy summer and a popular tourist attraction.
(US Army Corps of Engineers Collection)

Today's visitor center houses members of the Corps and comprehensive exhibits of local wildlife and the dam building process. *(Nancy Bell)*

Cabins now dot the area around Philpott and Fairy Stone lakes, constructed in remembrance of a simpler time. (*Nancy Bell*) Below, road construction was a big part of the early work of preparin for Philpott Lake. *(US Army Corps of Engineers Collection)*

Today's launching areas contain many more amenities. Above, Ryan's Branch in the early days. Below, Hurricane Agnes necessitated allowing reservoir levels to rise so that water did not breech the top of the dam. *(US Army of Corps of Engineers Collection)*

Construction of the first overlook in 1965.
(US Army Corps of Engineers Collection)

Ten Fast Facts about Philpott Dam

1. Philpott Dam is a gravity dam held in place by its own weight.

2. It is 90-feet long, 220-feet high and 166-feet wide.

3. There are 22 flights of stairways inside the dam – that is 287 steps to the top.

4. Since 1951, the dam has prevented an estimated $350 million in flood damage.

5. The amount of concrete used to construct Philpott Dam is enough to build 10 Washington monuments.

6. Philpott Dam is stronger today than when it was built – concrete strengthens with age.

7. Total cost of the dam, powerhouse, site clearing, relocations and land in the reservoir was nearly $14 million in 1953.

8. With three generators and a generating capacity of 14,000 kilowatts that is enough to provide power for 1,270 homes annually.

9. Philpott impounds a lake with almost 3,000 acres – nearly 200-feet deep in some places.

10. Water has never topped the spillway at an elevation of 985 feet. Record high in 1972 was 983 feet, and some spray crested the top of the dam and could be seen from behind.

--1980s brochure "Building Philpott Dam"

Today, a small marina exists near the Visitor's Center, to accommoda boaters.

Written Sources

Bassett Heritage Notes. Newsletter. Available at Bassett Historical Center.

Collection of Commonwealth of Virginia Highway Maps (1935, 1965). Franklin, Henry and Patrick Counties. Joe Yeaman, surveyor.

Esplin, Tracey A. *10,000 Years of History Buried Beneath Fairy Stone Lake: The Story of How Fairy Stone Lake Came to Be*. 48 Hour Books, 2009. Hardback book.

Hale, Hazel V. *Memories of Jamison Mill Era*. [Self-published, 1988]. Soft cover book.

Haynes, Elmer R. *The Fayerdale Tragedy at Fairy Stone State Park*. [Self-published, 1983]. Soft cover book.

Van Antrewp, RL. *The US Army Corps of Engineers: A History*. Alexandria VA, 2008. Softcover book.

Martinsville-Henry County Woman's Club. *Martinsville & Henry County Historic Views*. Hunter Publishing Co., Winston-Salem NC, 1976. Hardback book.

Monks, Matthew. *Philpott Anniversary, Role Celebrated: 'Sometimes Government Does Something Right.'* Martinsville Bulletin. Martinsville VA. 9/14/2003. Vol. 114, No. 221. Newspaper.

Wilson, John. *'Aunt Rosa' Opts for Convenience. Piedmont Profile*. Martinsville Bulletin. Martinsville VA. 10/16/1983.

Wooding III, Gl. *Dam Harnesses Former Food Waters*, Martinsville Bulletin. Martinsville Va. 9/11/1985. Vol. 96, Number 190. Newspaper.

Wooding III, Gl. *Dam's Unplanned Bonus Was Recreation on Lake*. Martinsville Bulletin. Martinsville VA. 9/12/85. Vol. 96, No. 191. Newspaper.

Wooding III, GI. *Potential Uses for Dam Include Lake Improvement.* Martinsville Bulletin. Martinsville VA. 9/13/85. Vol. 96, No. 192. Newspaper.

CCC newsletter, 1839 Speaks, Vol 2, No 3, December 1, 1939 –Fairy Stone State Park

ARCHAEOLOGICAL INVESTIGATIONS AT THE PHILPOTT SITE, HENRY COUNTY, VIRGINIA, R.P. Stephen David, Jr., Jane Eastman, and Thoma O. Maher. *Research Report No. 19, Research Laboratories of Archaeology, University of North Carolina at Chapel Hill, 1998.* Richard P. Gravely, Jr. was listed as an honorary author.

Interviews

Belcher, Douglas – Martinsville VA (numerous interviews regarding Native American culture and history in the area around Philpott Lake)

Hale, Hazel Via – Henry VA (numerous interviews re: history and photos of Jamison Mill area)

Haynes, Ronnie – Stuart VA (merchant records from time of Fayerdale Community)

Hodges, BK – Ferrum VA (former moonshine maker, transporter)

Kirkman, Eunice – Fairy Stone Park Highway VA (Native American history)

LaPrad, Dan – US Army Corps of Engineers at Philpott Lake (the Fayerdale Story)

Mabry, Louise S. – Fork Mountain VA (family history, father's drowning in Nicholas Creek)

Philpott, Charlie and JoAnne and their daughter, Patrice Newnam. Philpott VA (Story of the Philpott Family, naming of the lake, history of the area)

Philpott, Roger – Henry VA (His grandfather talked about the rising water on the family's former 300 acres around Salt House Branch)

Stephenson, Morris – Ferrum VA (Newspaper reporter, expert moonshining in Franklin County)

Rockwell, Craig – US Army Corps of Engineers, Philpott Lake (General history of the lake, plans for the future)

Yeaman, Joe – Patrick County VA (Virginia Highway maps 1932, 1950, 1965 and what the survey team saw)

Internet Sources

Civilian Conservation Corps 1938, 543th Co Camp Coos Head, Charleston, Oregon. History. http://freepages.genealogy.rootsweb.ancestry.com/~siskiyou/CampCc sHead.html

Heinemann. RL. Civilian Conservation Corps. (2012, January 18). In Encyclopedia Virginia. Retried from http://www.EncyclopediaVirginia.org/The_Civilian_Conservation_Corp com

Sullivan, Jack. *Those Whiskey Men*. http://www.pre-pro.com/jack_sullivan/index.php

Williamson, Jack. The Fayerdale Stave Mill. http://www.angelfire.com/folk/goblintown_mill/ StaveMill/StaveMill.html

Williamson, Jack. *A History of Fayerdale, Virginia*. http://www.angelfire.com/folk/goblintown_mill/ Fayerdale/Fayerdale.html

Williamson, Jack. *The Fayerdale Bandsaw Mill*. http://www.angelfire.com/folk/goblintown_mill/ SawMill/SawMill.htr

Index

A

ABC, 115, 116, 117
Archaeology, 20, 32, 33, 35, 144

B

Baliles, 29, 30
Barksdale, 41
Barnes, 14, 60
Barnett, 25
Bassett, 15, 16, 17, 19, 23, 31, 33, 59,
    66, 67, 75, 76, 78, 79, 80, 81, 89, 90,
    101, 107, 127, 129, 130, 131, 143
Bassett Historical Center, 16, 17, 19,
    23, 67, 81, 143
Bassett Mirror Company, 31, 78, 101
Belcher, 9, 22, 23, 26, 28, 145
Bell, 2, 3, 4, 13, 22, 38, 46, 48, 64, 66,
    82, 114, 124, 127, 128, 136, 137
Branch Creek, 59
Buchannan, 79
Burnette, 76

C

Carolina Road, 24
Carroll, 25
Carter, 10, 53, 55, 58, 61, 69, 70, 71,
    72, 73, 74
Catawba, 23, 32, 34
Cheraw, 23, 29, 31, 34
Cherokee, 23, 24, 25, 29
Civilian Conservation Corps, 47, 111,
    134, 146
Cooper, 59, 60
Cox, 76

D

Dan River, 2, 3, 4, 5, 6, 7, 8, 13, 24, 33,
    34, 132
Dan River Basin Association, 2, 3, 4, 5,
    6, 7, 8, 13, 132
Danville and Western, 45
DeHart, 10, 42, 77, 119, 122, 123
Delaware, 25
Depression, 9, 15, 54, 69, 70, 111, 121,
    133
Dodson, 47

F

Fain, 76
Fairy Stone State Park, 18, 111, 143
Fairystone, 9, 20, 25, 37, 38, 39, 46, 75,
    76, 78, 79, 91, 111, 112, 133, 135,
    144, 145
Farner, 79
Fayerdale, 38, 39, 41, 43, 44, 45, 46,
    47, 49, 59, 63, 66, 75, 76, 77, 78, 79,
    81, 121, 133, 134, 135, 143, 145,
    146
Fayerdale Tragedy, 121, 143
Ferrum, 71, 76, 113, 125, 126, 145
Fieldale, 19, 131
Fishburn, 41, 46, 134
Fleming, 119
Flood, 9, 15, 59, 130
Floyd, 7, 25, 131
Fort Detroit, 25
Franklin, 7, 15, 40, 41, 54, 89, 111, 113,
    115, 116, 117, 119, 121, 130, 143,
    145
French & Indians War, 25
Fugate, 45, 46

147

G

Garland, 81
Goblintown, 24, 25, 38, 39, 40, 41, 42, 45, 46, 47, 48, 75, 134
Goblintown Creek, 24, 25, 38, 39, 40, 42, 46, 47, 48, 75, 134
Goodwin, 41
Graham, 90
Gravely, 9, 31, 32, 33, 144
Gustin, 65

H

Hagood, 30
Hairston, 39, 41
Hale, 39, 42, 51, 53, 54, 55, 56, 57, 70, 71, 72, 74, 117, 143, 145
Halifax, 7, 25
Harris, 34
Helms, 10, 79, 81, 117
Henry, 2, 7, 15, 16, 33, 39, 43, 54, 70, 75, 79, 89, 113, 130, 143, 145
Herndon, 66, 91
Hill, 2, 32, 33, 41, 60, 144, 156
Hodges, 10, 124, 125, 126, 145
Hollandsworth, 76
Hurricane Agnes, 139

I

Iroquois, 24

J

Jamison Mill, 53, 54, 55, 56, 57, 58, 69, 70, 143, 145
Johnson, 73, 74, 77

K

Kirkman, 22, 29, 30, 31, 76, 145

L

Lafferty, 41
LaPrad, 133, 134, 135, 136, 145
Leffel, 92
Library of Congress, 34
Love, 117
Lovell, 77
Lunenburg, 25

M

Mabry, 59, 60, 62, 63, 64, 145
Maltese, 46
Martinsville, 2, 14, 23, 32, 33, 40, 67, 75, 81, 85, 131, 143, 144, 145
Mason, 90
Mayo River, 24
McGhee, 75
Mingo, 25
Mitchell, 89
Mize, 81
Moonshine, 10, 54, 113, 115, 117
Mount Airy, 44
Mountain Rose Distillery, 119, 123
Mullins, 61, 70

N

Native American, 9, 13, 15, 23, 26, 2' 33, 66, 145
New River, 25, 44
Nicholas Creek, 54, 55, 57, 62, 70, 7 72, 145
Norfolk and Western, 42, 44

O

Ohio, 25
Oklahoma, 31
Otter Creek, 25

P

Patrick, 7, 15, 24, 25, 29, 30, 31, 33, 35, 40, 41, 42, 45, 49, 54, 65, 67, 76, 77, 89, 112, 119, 143, 145
Peach Tree Bottom, 24
Philpott, 3, 5, 9, 10, 11, 12, 13, 14, 15, 16, 18, 20, 21, 23, 24, 25, 26, 29, 31, 32, 33, 34, 35, 37, 39, 42, 43, 45, 51, 53, 55, 59, 60, 65, 67, 68, 69, 72, 75, 76, 77, 78, 79, 80, 81, 82, 83, 85, 87, 88, 89, 91, 92, 98, 99, 101, 104, 106, 110, 111, 113, 119, 121, 123, 127, 128, 129, 130, 131, 133, 135, 136, 137, 138, 141, 143, 145, 151
Philpott Dam, 11, 13, 16, 18, 76, 81, 92, 98, 104, 110, 131, 141
Philpott Lake, 5, 10, 13, 18, 24, 26, 29, 34, 35, 39, 42, 51, 53, 55, 60, 67, 68, 69, 75, 79, 91, 99, 106, 111, 113, 121, 127, 128, 129, 130, 131, 133, 137, 138, 145, 151
Plecker, 29, 31
Prillaman, 40, 58, 59, 113
Prohibition, 15, 45, 77, 119, 121, 133
Pusey, 25

R

Ramsey, 4, 104, 105, 106, 108, 138
Republican School, 60
Roanoke, 7, 24, 43, 44, 81, 82, 89, 134
Robertson, 29, 30
Rockwell, 10, 128, 129, 130, 131, 132, 135, 145
Roman, 46
Roosevelt, 111
Rorrer, 59
Runnett Bag Creek, 113

S

Saint Andrews, 46
Salt House Branch, 77, 145
Saura, 23, 24, 34
Shady Rest, 66
Shawnee, 25
Shelton, 60, 63, 121
Shooting Creek, 113
Smith, 7, 13, 15, 16, 17, 19, 23, 24, 25, 32, 33, 34, 40, 42, 44, 45, 54, 59, 65, 71, 76, 79, 81, 89, 91, 93, 94, 99, 103, 108, 109, 116, 117, 121, 131
Smith River, 13, 15, 16, 17, 19, 23, 24, 25, 32, 33, 34, 40, 42, 45, 54, 59, 71, 79, 81, 89, 91, 93, 99, 103, 108, 109, 121, 131
Stegall, 77
Stephenson, 114, 115, 116, 117, 145
Stone, 10, 18, 41, 46, 82, 111, 112, 127, 134, 136, 143
Stovall, 41
Stuart's Knob, 39, 41, 44, 47, 133

T

Trout, 40
Turner, 35, 40
Tutelo, 24

U

Union Bridge, 47
Union Iron Works, 39, 40, 41, 134
University of North Carolina, 20, 32, 33, 35, 144
US Army Corps of Engineers, 5, 13, 18, 65, 92, 93, 94, 95, 96, 98, 99, 100, 101, 102, 103, 107, 109, 127, 132, 133, 137, 138, 140, 143, 145
USS MERRIMAC, 41

149

V

Virginia Canals and Navigations
   Society, 40
Virginia Museum of Natural History, 23
Virginia Ore and Lumber, 41, 46, 79,
   134
VO&L, 41, 43, 44

W

Warrior's Path, 24

West Piedmont Planning District
   Commission, 67, 110
Williamson, 39, 50, 133, 134, 146
Woolwine, 42, 77, 119
Workman, 25
Wyandotte, 25

Y

Yeaman, 64, 65, 66, 67, 143, 145
Young, 76

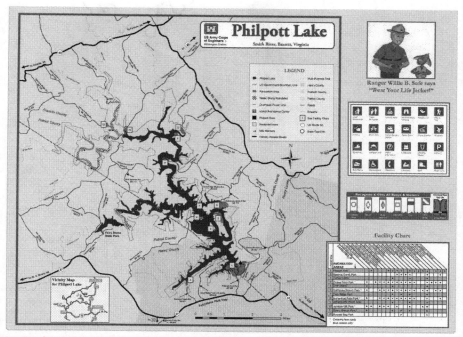

Today's Philpott Lake contains a number of parks and recreation areas.

Philpott Lake

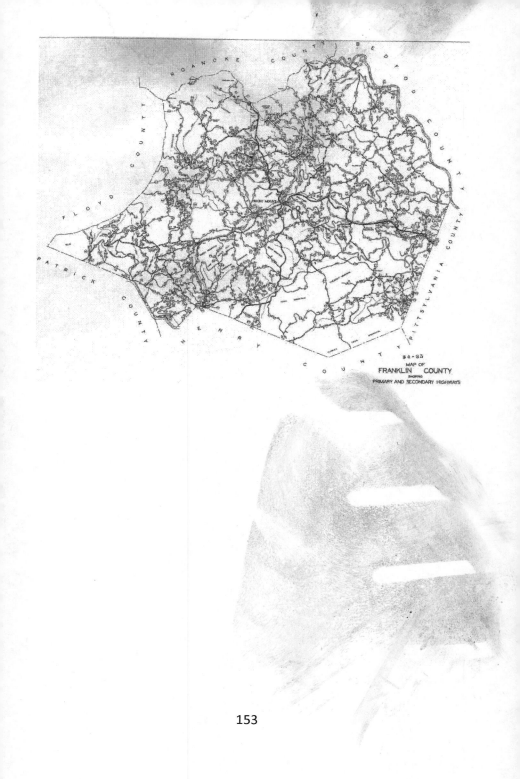

34-35

MAP OF
FRANKLIN COUNTY
SHOWING
PRIMARY AND SECONDARY HIGHWAYS

153

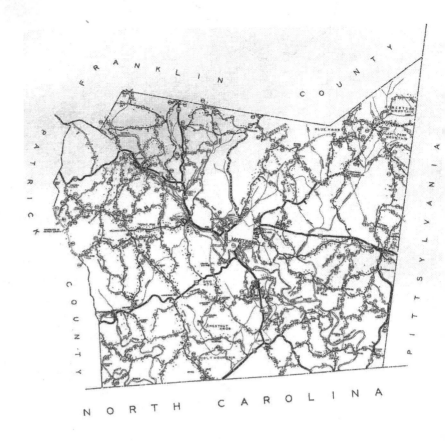

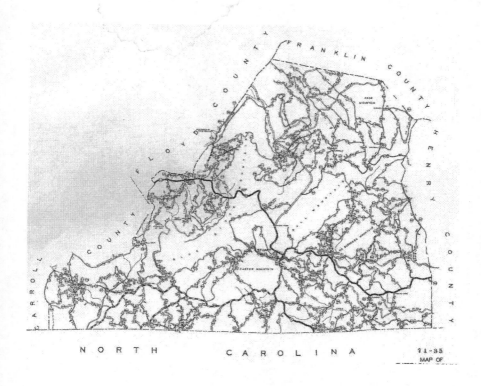

This book published by Tom Perry's Laurel Hill Publishing LLC
4443 Ararat Highway
P. O. Box 11
Ararat, VA 24053
freestateofpatrick@yahoo.com
276-692-5300

www.freestateofpatrick.com

Publisher Acknowledgements

Tom Perry's Laurel Hill Publishing LLC would like to acknowledge the assistance of Jennifer Gregory, Debbie Hall, Cindy Headen, Jo Anne Philpott, Pat Ross, and the staff of the Bassett Historical Center.

Made in the USA
Charleston, SC
25 October 2015